# DOING TIME WITH MY SON

A MOTHER AND SON'S STORY OF ENDURING LOVE THROUGH INCARCERATION

**BETTYE L. BLAIZE**
**TERRENCE G. WHITE**

FULL CIRCLE PRESS

Copyright 2016 by Bettye L. Blaize and Terrence G. White

Published by Full Circle Press

ALL RIGHTS RESERVED

No part of this book may be reproduced in any form or by any means without the prior written permission of Bettye Blaize, except brief quotes used in connection with reviews written specifically for inclusion in a magazine, newspaper, or electronic review, in which case attribution, including the primary author's name, is required.

Printed in the United States of America

**FULL CIRCLE PRESS**
700 E. Redlands Blvd, Suite U #293
Redlands, CA 92373
Cataloging-in-Publication data for this book is available from the
Library of Congress

978-0-9976032-3-1    3172017

Copies of this book are available at special discounts for bulk purchases in the U.S. by schools, non-profit organizations, and other government and private agencies. For more information, please contact the Special Markets Department, Full Circle Press at 700 E. Redlands Blvd, Ste U #293, Redlands, CA 92373 or at www.fullcirclepress.org.

Cover design and layout by Laura Marie

This is a work of nonfiction. Personal events are portrayed to the best of the authors' memories. All stories shared represent the viewpoints of those interviewed and are not necessarily representative of the authors' viewpoints or experiences. The information contained in this book is for informational purposes only and should not be used to replace the specialized training and professional judgment of a mental health professional, substance abuse counselor, or any other professional. The reader should consult with his/her doctor in any matters pertaining to his/her health and should consult a physician or a trained mental health professional before making any decision regarding treatment of self or others. This book is not meant to be used, nor should it be used, to diagnose or treat any medical condition. It is sold with the understanding that neither the authors nor publisher are engaged to render any type of medical, psychological, or other professional advice. Neither the publisher nor the authors shall be held liable for any physical, psychological, emotional, financial, or commercial damages, including but not limited to special, incidental, consequential, or other damage.

# DOING TIME WITH MY SON

A MOTHER AND SON'S STORY OF ENDURING LOVE THROUGH INCARCERATION

Love heals. Heals and liberates. I use the word love, not meaning sentimentality, but a condition so strong that it may be that which holds the stars in their heavenly positions and that which causes the blood to flow orderly in our veins.

— Maya Angelou

# **DEDICATION**

To every boy and young man of purpose who is destined for greatness, regardless of your current circumstances. Find a dream, claim it, and make it yours. This book is dedicated to your lives and your dreams. We believe in you.

And to the mothers and grandmothers who love them. Where there is hope, there is a future. Through your selfless love and your unwavering faith, you are helping to ensure a better future for us all. This book belongs to you and to that hope.

# CONTENTS

Foreword by Dr. LaMarr Darnell Shields..................................................xiii
Prologue by Terrence G. White.................................................................xvii
Introduction by Bettye L. Blaize..............................................................xxi

Book One: Letters of Love

   Part I: Before

      Chapter 1: The Early Years.......................................................5
      Chapter 2: Family Secrets........................................................ 11
      Chapter 3: Don't Blink............................................................ 25
      Chapter 4: Up All Night, Asleep All Day............................. 35
      Chapter 5: Highs and Lows.................................................... 43

   Part II: During

      Chapter 6: The Waiting Room ............................................. 49
      Chapter 7: Settling In.............................................................. 57
      Chapter 8: The Cards............................................................. 67
      Chapter 9: The Promise.......................................................... 71

   Part III: After

      Chapter 10: Freedom.............................................................. 77
      Chapter 11: Re-Entry............................................................... 81
      Chapter 12: Family Man......................................................... 91

Lessons for Mothers, Young Men, and Service Providers............................97

Book Two: The Village

   Introduction and Editor's Note.....................................................121
   Part I: The Family Village.............................................................123
   Part II: The Community Village...................................................173

Book Three: Wisdom from the Inside
    Introduction and Editor's Note ....................................................... 199
    The Wisdom .................................................................................. 203
Epilogue by Terrence G. White ........................................................ 251
Gratitude ............................................................................................ 253
About the Authors ............................................................................. 256
About Full Circle Press ..................................................................... 258

# FOREWORD

## DR. LAMARR DARNELL SHIELDS

When I was growing up on the Southside of Chicago, it was pretty common knowledge amongst me and my friends that if you didn't finish high school and have a plan for your life, you would most certainly end up on a fast track to trouble. Knowing this, I have to question why so many of my friends got caught up in gangs and/or drugs, even though we came from such strong families and knew better. Although I was never enticed by drugs or gangs, I was not immune to many of the other social ills that my single mother attempted to shield me from. Even so, I managed to go on to earn my BA degree, my master's degree, and eventually my Ph.D.

Given this reality, I've long thought my success — like that of many other young men growing up in violent cities without male guidance — was the result of my own hard work and perseverance. However, after reading *Doing Time with my Son* and comparing Terrence's story with my own, I began to question at a deeper level if maybe in some ways I was more privileged than I had realized. I was not privileged over Terrence when it came to money, family support, and access to decent Catholic schools, but somewhere along the line I was able to escape what he was not, and that alone means that I was afforded opportunities that Terrence — until very recently — never saw.

As a parent, it's only human nature to blame yourself when your own child strays into what you worked so hard to shield him from. So many mothers — Black, Brown, and White — who have sung the same song of "Where did I go wrong?" for years will find refuge in the words in this book. Even though Bettye often felt lonely during the journey she took with her son through incarceration, in her heart she knew that she wasn't. For those of you who are reading this and feel that you have found yourself at a crossroads similar to Bettye's, know that you are not alone and that hope is on the horizon.

When you have a child in prison, it is understandably hard to talk with others about your situation. There was a time when Bettye thought she couldn't tell anyone about her son's incarceration because she didn't want herself, her son, and her family to be judged because of it. She was embarrassed by her situation and thought that the burden she carried had to be shouldered alone. It takes courage to tell this story with such honesty and candor, so as you read it, don't judge the voices and experiences of the authors, their family members and friends, and other men currently serving time. Most importantly, don't judge yourself.

This is a book that has been a long time coming. It comes at a time when prison rates for men of color continue to climb at astronomical and disproportionate rates. Currently, the incarceration rate in the United States of America is the highest in the world. The over-incarceration of males of color, specifically African American and Latino males, has created alarming challenges for families throughout this nation. This toll of incarceration can be measured by escalating levels of poverty and increase in crime and substance abuse among youth and family members. According to the Department of Justice, America's prison population exceeds two million inmates.

By 2002, America's jails held 1 in every 142 U.S. citizens. The issue of incarceration and its impact on families is so severe that Congress authorized millions of federal dollars to create special programs to support children ages 4 to 18 who have an incarcerated parent. If we are ever going to overcome this societal phenomenon that is both a public health and a social justice issue, we're going to have to take the time to open our hearts, minds, and lives to stories like the ones told here.

As I travel across the country speaking in churches, schools, and other arenas with Bettye in tow, I often ask her to share her story with audiences waiting to hear me speak. Whenever she takes the mic, she most always steals the show. I'm so glad that she has finally decided to put her story down so that you, too, can feel what so many others have felt anytime she's shared her story.

There's a scripture in Jeremiah 31:16 that reads, "Thus says the Lord: 'Refrain your voice from weeping, and your eyes from tears; for your work shall be rewarded, and they shall come back from the land of the enemy. There is hope in your future, that your children shall come back to their own border.'" *Doing Time with My Son* is an educational narrative about struggle, triumph, and forgiveness during one of the darkest times of Bettye's life. May the pages that follow encourage you to be hopeful no matter your current situation, empathetic to human conditions whether they lie within or beyond your scope of experience, and inspired to use your own story to positively impact the lives of others.

# PROLOGUE

## TERRENCE G. WHITE

### SUMMER 2006

I'm writing this from a prison cell, wondering where this story should start and where it's going to end. I guess the only place I can really start this story, or any story, is with my mother and grandmother. I was raised by two strong women. The best of who I am is because of who they are. They loved me with a fierceness borne of their belief that loving unconditionally was the only path they could travel alongside me on this journey.

In many ways, I had everything that I could have asked for as a young child. All my needs and more were met. Yet I was led to the streets in search of a way to fill an emptiness that I felt so desperately after my father, stepfather, and grandfather all died within a short timeframe. Even though I didn't find the deep love I needed on the streets, what I found did manage to fill the void. I found male figures who were willing to give me attention and guidance, no matter how misguided and messed up it may have been. I also found a way to numb the pain, an anesthetic to shut out all that I knew about what it meant to live right in this world. But what I found on the streets, no matter how exciting it may have seemed at the time, didn't hold a candle to all I lost in the process. I lost my youth. I lost the plan for my life that my mother had worked so hard to guide me toward. I lost my way.

I know now that no matter how much I might want to turn back time, I can't get those years back. My youth is gone, and as I sit here writing this from a prison cell, I know that no amount of freedom I may have felt on the streets was worth the true freedom that I lost. I lost my compass of what it meant to do right and live right – the roadmap that my mother and grandmother had given me throughout my life. And without this compass, I made bad choices not just once or twice, but over and over and over again.

I believe now, sitting here as a 35-year-old man, that if I had used the tools my mother and grandmother had given me early in life, I would not be writing this from a prison cell. And yet I also know that this place has saved my life. I can't look back on my life with regret, because everything that's happened to me – all the choices I've made, both good and bad – have brought me to this moment in time and are going to carry me through. If it weren't for the life I lived, I wouldn't have been given the beautiful gift of my first daughter when I was only 15 years old. And the love of my life, Brandee, came into my world at a time when everything else seemed to be crumbling around me. So these lights in my life, these examples of what real love looks like in action, were the rays of sun during an otherwise very dark time.

I didn't realize it or appreciate it as a child, but now I can look back and be so grateful for the way my mom raised me as far with manners. She trained me to be a responsible man, even though I didn't use what she taught me right away. Now that I'm older, I can see how she laid a strong foundation and instilled in me a solid work ethic. Just watching the way she worked taught me a lot. I'm her son all the way.

## PROLOGUE

I could say "I'm sorry" a thousand times and it wouldn't be enough. And yet I'm going to say it over and over again. More than speaking the words, though, I want my life from here on out to be the best apology letter, the greatest love letter that I could ever write. I want my *life* and the choices I make to speak nothing but love and redemption.

To the young men out there who feel lost, there *is* hope and there are people who really care and want you to succeed in life. Even though life is going to test you, you can rise above the mess. Prison is the worst place in the world; don't let anyone ever tell you differently. Someone controls your every minute. There is no freedom here, no life. I have two pairs of pants, two shirts, and one pair of shoes. I have nothing but me, which means I have to face myself everyday. I have learned to be humble and stay out of harm's way. I have learned patience and how to walk away from trouble instead of toward it. I had to learn that in order to become the person I am today. Today, I make good choices with respect to who I socialize with.

In these past years, I have had to dig deep and find out about Terrence. I have learned the difference between good and bad. It is important that we find out who we are and what makes us tick. I love me today and that is so important because if you don't love yourself it will be very hard to love or care about anyone else. Today I care about everyone's feelings. This is the new and improved me. I know things are only going to get better from here.

# INTRODUCTION
## BETTYE L. BLAIZE

*Doing Time with My Son* is an autobiographical narrative of my journey with my son, Terrence, leading up to, during, and after his multiple incarcerations, the longest of which lasted nearly a decade, coupled with some perspectives from the village that surrounded us and continues to lift us up. This book also includes a powerful collection of insights written by inmates serving time in and around the Maryland area. I've called Baltimore home my entire life. It's where I raised my son and where I now am watching my granddaughters, great-granddaughter, and great-grandsons grow up. So it was only fitting that I kept this project, which is so close to my heart and sense of purpose, close to home.

The stories, though — my own, my son's, my family's and friends', and those of the men and mothers who were willing to share their experiences and knowledge for this project — are universal. They're both a reflection of the humanity inherent in all of us and also a unique look into the lives of those caught up in the criminal justice system. You'll see a lot of hope in the pages that follow, but you'll also see the hopelessness inherent in the devastation and destruction that prison and jails wreak on families. The wise words of a man who is currently serving a life sentence, for example, can only bring so much hope when we know that the wisdom he has to share only applies to his own life in hindsight.

I've worked to relay my own experiences as honestly as possible. I'm a mother first, though, and so when it comes to the journey of my own son and the time he served, I have to tell the story of my son first and of the inmate second.

This is a book for families, community leaders, and other stakeholders who are truly concerned about the impact of incarceration on individuals and families. I've tried to paint a clear picture of the day-to-day struggles of maintaining some semblance of a normal life when my son was locked up, but it wasn't always easy. It impacted me and my family economically, physically, and — of course — emotionally.

If you are reading this and have never experienced first-hand the incarceration of yourself or of a loved one, my hope is that this book gives you an empathetic, but realistic, look at a struggle that has become a national crisis. And if you are reading this as a family member of an inmate or an inmate yourself, my hope is that the words on the pages that follow help give voice to a struggle that you know only too well. If I've learned anything from my own journey, it's that together we can always move forward with hope, knowing that no matter where we come from, what we've been through, and what lies ahead, love endures.

# BOOK ONE
# LETTERS OF LOVE

BEING DEEPLY LOVED BY SOMEONE GIVES
YOU STRENGTH, WHILE LOVING SOMEONE DEEPLY
GIVES YOU COURAGE.

– LAO TZU

# PART I
# BEFORE

IN THEIR INNOCENCE, CHILDREN KNOW THEMSELVES TO BE LIGHT AND LOVE. IF WE WILL ALLOW THEM, THEY CAN TEACH US TO SEE OURSELVES THE SAME WAY.
— MICHAEL JACKSON

# 1
# THE EARLY YEARS

Dear Son,

I gave birth to you, my one and only son, five months after my 21st birthday. I named you Terrence Gregory White and from the moment you were first born I thought you were nothing but perfect. Even though there's so much that you didn't get to share with your father throughout his time here on Earth, you did share his birthday.

I was in the eleventh grade at Douglas High School when I met your father. I was a terrible student and honestly didn't go to school much at all – we spent more time out of school than in. Even though I wasn't a good student, I knew that I had to live up to the expectation of my mother. The promise in my mother's house was that everybody was going to graduate. At that time, the graduations were held at the Civic Center and my mom told all of us that she didn't care how long it took us, everybody was getting a diploma and we were all walking across that Civic Center stage. We all did, of course.

Everyone called my mother Gran and my father Big Dad. Speaking of Gran, I know you remember as well as I do the feeling of walking into her house. You'd walk in the door and just never want to leave. There was always something cooking and it always seemed like an old person's house, even when I was coming up as a kid. Everyone's picture was on the wall in a frame, with no design to the arrangement of frames whatsoever. How she had all these pictures without ever owning a camera, I'll never know. We called it the wall of shame — when I'd look at those pictures as I grew I'd say, "Ma, you need to take this photo down" and she'd say, "No, that was you."

Whatever Mama was cooking, she was going to make you eat some *and* take some home. Whatever she gave you, she wrapped it in aluminum foil — money, can of soda, everything. Everybody loved Gran's mac and cheese — if she cut some for me, she would say, "No, it's Bettye's" and if I was gone for a couple of days or more, she'd freeze it. As you know, I went to my mother's house every single Sunday and had dinner with her until she passed. My gas tank was always on empty and Gran would always ask if I had gas and then would give me five dollars and tell me to fill the tank.

Gran and my two sisters had great green thumbs and they used to pinch off each other's plants. And yet if anyone took anything from Gran's house, she always knew. Even though it was just her and my father in the house, she always bought everything in bulk — toilet paper all the way to the ceiling. And yet if even one roll went missing, she would know it. I used to steal aluminum foil and toilet paper.

Everything happened at Gran's house — Thanksgiving, Christmas, and all the other holidays. Gran cooked every Sunday after church and her house was the place to be. Everyone would just show up, knowing they'd be guaranteed a good meal. I used to bring the construction crew from work home to my mother's. She never would say no when it came to feeding a person. Never. So we all had the best of the world at my mother's house.

Gran watched you and all of the other kids — not one of you ever had a babysitter. She took you to school and picked you up and was pretty much the primary influence in your early life because I worked so much. She instilled something in each one of you. You still hear them sharing memories when we're all together, "Gran said..."

She called you "Poot" and really loved you something fierce. She always reached out to the children who were in need. The kids who were doing okay, she did for them, too. But she had a soft spot for those of you who struggled. Your cousin Dink remembers it like this: "I asked Gran to get me a book for college and she didn't get it for me, but then she'd always send you money for your commissary." Gran said the ones in the family who needed her help were the ones she was going to help. She would have a list for her bills and anyone who was in jail was on that list. If they weren't in jail and they needed money, she would wrap that money in aluminum foil and put it in the mailbox. She always had for all of us.

My father was a man of few words, but you kids all adored Big Dad. He was everything you'd want your child to be around in a man. He would sit on the back porch and watch all the neighborhood kids going to and coming home from school. Every day he'd watch them walk by, one by one, until the one day he said, "Nobody's walking down the alley no more, everybody's driving." Whatever Gran did, Big Dad would just follow her lead

As you know, I was the baby of the family. My mother, though she didn't have much formal education herself, was a smart lady and always insisted on us focusing on school. She said that school was the whole thing, the only thing we needed to focus on when we were younger. Both of my sisters, your aunts, were honors students, so they didn't need any push. They just came home, did their work, and that was that. For me, just barely passing everything was the only academic honor I could brag about. But Gran always said that as long as we did our best, that was good enough for her. She never compared me to my sisters when it came to school — she just pushed us all to do our best.

Gran always insisted on us being young ladies and trained us up in the foundation of what that looked like. She was a socialite and I remember going to cabarets with her and Big Dad when I was only 13. They didn't believe in leaving their children with anyone, so we got to dress up and go out to the social events with them. She was a lady and she taught us to be ladies. And just being with my father taught us what a man should look like. If Big Dad didn't do anything else, he loved his girls right, my mom included. My father taught us what we should look for in a husband and a father for our children.

So we had a very wholesome upbringing, all things considered. My mother taught us to base our wealth on our own income because, as she always made sure we understood, no man was promised forever. And as we left home to go out on our own, my father taught us that the man who raised you, provided for you, and nurtured you should never put his hands on you.

• • •

## THE EARLY YEARS

Dear Mom,

I know that when you were growing up in East Baltimore, it really was the village. Everyone looked out for each other and each other's children. As you've told me, there was no such thing as privacy — it was any parent's right to be up in any child's business at any time. If you acted out, there was some adult around to set you straight, each and every time. By the time I was born, there was still some semblance of the village intact, but things were changing quickly. By the time I hit my teenage years, kids were calling 911 on parents and adults started to act afraid of their own children. I can see how you feel that many of these changes weren't positive ones because once parents became afraid to discipline their own children, they really began to feel like they were losing control.

Along with the erosion of the village, you also told me that the neighborhoods started to disintegrate. Suddenly, there became no consequences for what young people did. Once the dynamics of the neighborhood started to change, people started minding their own business. When you were growing up, nobody had their own "private" business — if you got in trouble in school, you got in trouble at home. Once the neighborhood stopped being the village, it just became housing. And that's what's still going on — the consequences seem so low. You see people killing people in broad daylight — at a corner where there are always people — and nobody says anything.

Maybe this is why when I decided where I was going to raise my own family, I chose to live in the suburbs in the county. I never really lived in the city-city where you grew up though, because when I was very young we moved out of Gran's house to our home that you bought in a nice area. At the end of the day I don't know how much it mattered — because whatever trouble I sought, I found. Even if I had to travel a little farther to get it. But I'm getting ahead of myself here. We haven't even gotten to how you and my father met, so maybe we should get to that part first.

# 2
# FAMILY SECRETS

Dear Son,

I met your father through his brother, who was a classmate and the boyfriend of my best girlfriend. Most of the time we hooked school and went to the boyfriend's house. I had never really had a steady boyfriend before your dad. We just started talking from the first day we met at his childhood home, and from that point on every time he came home on leave he would call me and we'd spend as much time as possible together, until he was sent to Vietnam. Your father and his best friend had enlisted in the Army on the buddy-buddy plan and he did one tour in Vietnam. We had been dating a year at the time and decided to stay together and just write back and forth to each other while he was away.

I didn't tell you this when you were younger, but your father came back from Vietnam a different man. Most of the guys who returned from Vietnam in the early '70s came home with some type of addiction and your father was no exception. He developed a drug addiction that he just couldn't shake. When he first came home, he was sent to Walter Reed Hospital in D.C. for a 30-day rehab program. He got clean and appeared to be okay, but his sobriety didn't last for long. Vietnam changed something deep inside of him. He was the nicest dude ever when we met, the greatest man out of the whole bunch of guys. But he came back from war angry, haunted, broken.

By the time I thought I couldn't take it anymore and decided to break it off with him, I was already pregnant, even though I didn't know it at the time. You were conceived on New Year's Eve of 1971, in a motel room. There's not much more to it than that. I was already disconnected from him by the time I got pregnant, but still saw him because I had developed a relationship with his family by this time. I think the final breaking point for me was the time when I actually saw him get high. It was one thing to see the effects of the drugs, but when I saw him shooting heroin, that was it. I had watched so many of my friends become a part of the drug scene by staying with guys who were using, but I knew that that wasn't going to be an option for me. So I just left. We never lived together, as I was still living at Gran's house and he was at his family's house.

He was excited when he found out you were going to be born, but I already knew that he wasn't going to be physically and mentally available to go through it all with me. He didn't come to doctor appointments or anything. I had a lot of support, though, from both my family and his. To this day I have relationships with his one brother who's still alive and with his cousins. Your father was a good father when you were born and did the best he could. He wasn't a hands-on father, but I believe he was the best he could be. His family loved you so much and even though he was deep into his own addiction, you went to your grandparents' house on the weekends from the time you were a baby and your father would always be with you on those visits.

We were so young – I graduated from high school and you were born a few months after that. I was six months pregnant when I graduated. My father never said much of anything, but my mother was really not feeling it, so to say. That being said, by the time everyone knew I was pregnant it was too late for me to do anything except to have the baby. She still insisted that I was going to go to school and get that diploma. At that time, if the high school found out you were pregnant they would send you to this special school, but they never caught me so I was able to finish school and graduate with a regular diploma. By the time you were born, Gran had gotten over it and just knew we had a child who needed to be taken care of and that's what she was going to do.

I went back to school for cosmetology when you were only a few months old. Gran watched you during the day, but I would get you up and dressed every morning before I headed to school. Gran made sure that I was responsible for doing what I needed to do as your mother. She was very clear that she was not a babysitting service and that she would only watch you when I was at school or work. You were such a laid back baby and everybody in the family loved to watch you because you never caused anyone any trouble. You rarely cried, slept through the night, and were just such a joy to be around.

Your father was 36 or so when he died from an overdose. You were only 9. I remember your grandmother calling with the news and my fiancé and me taking you out to dinner to tell you that your father had passed. You were sad and hurt because you did have a connection with your father, even though he wasn't around all the time. I know there's a lot you probably weren't able to process because we didn't go into the details of any of it. Looking back now, I think that maybe sometime before you turned 15 years old I should have told you the truth about the circumstances of his death. I think that you should have known the whole story.

• • •

Dear Mom,

I did all the right things as a child, I think. Things to make you proud. I was a good athlete and played baseball, football and basketball. I loved sports with all my heart. I played the drums in the school band and I actually enjoyed my day-to-day life coming up. You have told me many times that I was different from a lot of the other boys around our neighborhood, never causing any problems and rarely, if ever, getting myself into trouble.

You tell me that I was only four years old when I first picked up a baseball bat and that my love for the sport was instantaneous. You tell me that you used to get such joy from going out to the ballpark to watch me play t-ball, and then later baseball. I used to tell you that I was going to make it to the pros one day, but I guess God had some different plans for my life.

We lived with Gran, Big Dad, and one of my aunts and cousins until I was about five years old. Even though I don't have too many memories from those early years, you tell me that life was good. I know that my dad lived nearby and that I spent a lot of time with him and his parents, my grandparents. I know we lived in Northeast Baltimore, a nice community full of row houses owned by proud home-owning families. It was a good place to grow up. I know that when I was five years old, we moved into our own home just ten minutes from your parents' house. We lived in a two-bedroom townhouse — welcoming and comfortable. You worked hard to make our home a place where I, and anyone else who walked through the door, knew that they were loved. You tell me that I didn't want to leave Gran's house, but that once I realized that this new place was going to be our home, I thrived. There were a lot of other kids in the complex who I became good friends with and I loved being able to have my friends over to play.

You tell me that I always liked school and that I was a social kid who thrived in math. You tell me that you remember vividly walking me to school on the first day of first grade, me all decked out in my Catholic school uniform and Sebagos with a backpack that seemed almost as big as I was. Even though I was such a jokester, I never got into any trouble in those early years.

When I was eight or nine years old, I joined the basketball team. I also played baseball and football for the Northwood League. I remember the day that I played a doubleheader as a pitcher in the All Star game and the home run that I made at the end of the first game. I slid into third base and hit my knee, but continued on and played in the second game. You said that you kept watching me limp, but that I kept telling you that I was fine. And you told me that if it really didn't hurt, I needed to prove it to you by running up the alley and then running back down. Later that evening, my aunts took me to the hospital and we discovered that I actually had a broken knee that needed a full cast. I had somehow managed to play through that second game and even helped my team to the win.

As for my dad, the memories I have with him fit into a very small window, but I do remember him being a good person. When I was small, I remember one Christmas when he came with all these presents that I probably couldn't use for a couple of years yet, like a 10-speed bike. I remember him coming to one of my baseball games, and all I knew was that he was my dad and I was his son and I loved him. I'm grateful that I knew his family and that they knew me. Of course when I was little I never knew he had a problem. I remember being with him a couple of weeks before he passed away. I'm not going to sit here and say he didn't teach me anything, it's just that my time with him was so brief. I do have one story, though, that I want to share, from later on in life. It's about Dad, so I want to tell it here. One day when I was in prison, the guard came to get me and take me to court. He called my name on the cell block and when I walked up to him he just stood there and stared at me, not saying anything for a good minute. I asked him what was wrong, and he just said, "I don't know. I heard your last name and you just resemble him so much." He was like, "Man, was your father's name Terry White?" I said, "Yeah" and then he went on to tell me this whole story about my father's life, including what he was like coming up. The guard then introduced me to some guys in prison who had known my father, and they all told me that my father was a good man who was loved by everyone. They said he was friendly and was just a good person who went to Vietnam and got mentally all messed up with drugs. They all told me that I was just like him.

• • •

Dear Son,

By the time your father passed away, I had been with Blaize for a few years. We got married on July 14, 1984 and less than two years later — on April 19, 1986 — he was gone. He died of a brain aneurism. And then just a few short months later, in September, your grandfather died. You were only 14 years old. So much loss in such a short amount of time. The Sunday before Blaize died, I remember that I was at work when he punished you for some thing or another. You were mad about it, so you called Gran to come get you. Blaize said that he wasn't going to open the door for Gran and that his punishment was going to stand whether you liked it or not. You were mad, saying that you wanted to go back and live with Gran. Yet just a couple short days later, you had made friends again with Blaize and gotten past your disagreement — I'm sure it had something to do with you wanting to go out with your friends and him thinking otherwise. Two days later, Blaize was dead. He wasn't sick at the time. He had even gone to work that morning. I remember he called and told me he had a headache and was going home. When I got home, he wasn't there and I knew immediately that something was wrong. The phone was off the hook and I could see where he had thrown up. By the time I got to the hospital, he had already passed away. I found out later that he had run out of the house and had fallen between two cars. The police thought he was drunk or high or something, so they didn't really treat him the way I thought they should have.

I didn't go back to work for about six months. I was a wreck. Before he was my husband, he was my best friend. I couldn't get myself together. My friend Sherrie came and stayed with us for weeks. I knew I had to get it together because I still had you to raise, but I'd be lying if I didn't say that it was really hard for me. Even after a year had passed and I started to regain some normalcy, there were certain times that I just shut down. When he died, I really felt like I had died with him. Nothing mattered to me anymore. I was never that girl who dreamed of her wedding day or who always wanted to get married — it just happened that

I met a person who completed me.

He was the kindest man I've ever known and was everything that I could have wanted in a partner. There wasn't anything spectacular about him, honestly. He was good looking, but it wasn't that. It was just something about him that moved me. Before him, I was a receiver. I was the 19-year-old girl with full diamonds and mink coats, always thinking that that's what I needed from a man to be happy. And yet when I met Blaize, all that changed. He had nothing more than I did, but there was just something really different about him from the beginning.

As you know, we met one night at the Holiday Inn. My girlfriends and I had gone out drinking and I remember seeing him and telling my girlfriend that I thought he was kind of cute and that I thought he was going to be my husband. The next day he called the hotel where I was working to ask about a banquet. I asked if it was Mr. Blaize on the line and he said that it was. I then told him that I knew that he wasn't really looking for a banquet. He asked me out and I told him that my girlfriends and I were going to come through. From that night on, we were together. I remember he told me early on that my mother and father and sisters and brothers and all the men before him had spoiled me, so that he didn't have to do a thing. And he was telling the truth – he didn't give me anything that first Christmas. He challenged me in a lot of good ways, and I think he was sent to me for a purpose. I wouldn't get my hands dirty for anything before I met him, but something about the way he loved me made me want to be more independent. Before him, I just expected people to take care of me. He turned me into the self-sufficient woman I am today. I still miss him every day.

• • •

Dear Mom,

As for Blaize, I loved that man. He was everything to me. Things were a little rocky in the beginning because I was just a kid when he stepped in as a father figure. He wasn't my father, though, and I knew that, so the whole situation took a little getting used to. I can honestly say that he is the one who taught me how to be a man coming up. Even when I started to run with a lot of rough guys, I was always the one who had a little bit of class. I knew how to conduct myself around people, how to use knives and forks properly, how to knot a tie. He also taught me how to treat a woman because I watched how he treated you. I always took notice — how he brought you flowers and wine, cooked dinner, and took care of me as if I was his own son.

I have memories of doing a lot of things with Blaize — just the two of us. Every time I had a game he would leave his job and run out to the ballpark so I could see him on the baseball field in his suit and tie and then he'd run back to work. I know that you both made it a point to get there so that I could look up in the stands and see you and know that you were present and that you cared. I also remember going with Blaize to the Civic Center to watch professional wrestling matches together.

But through my whole childhood, I never had a stable male in my life who stayed. You married when I was young and I loved Blaize and I have to give thanks to him for showing me what it means to love someone, because he loved you and I saw it every day until he passed away. And yet all the important men in my life died within two years of each other and this left me so lost, more so than I ever realized at the time. I didn't see all the damage this loss did to me until recently. I was scared deeply because I loved these men. I know my father loved me, but at some point I think he must have loved the drugs more.

Speaking of my father, I want to thank you for not talking badly about him. Because of this, I saw my father as a good man when I was a child. I now know that he was a good man with a disease. He was an addict. And yet I think just the fact that I didn't have a stable role model around all of the time left me broken. As I grew I realized that I could take advantage of you and Gran maybe more than I would have a father. I know this might be hard to understand because you were strict with me, but I see a similar thing with my younger daughter – her mom can say something to her five times and she doesn't respond or tries to argue and then I say the same thing to her one time and she listens.

I remember that things were different when Blaize was still around. Even though he wasn't my father biologically, he was your husband and I respected him. I know you raised me well and did the best you could, but there were some things that you said as a woman that if they had come from a man may have come across totally different. And I don't want to seem disrespectful or ungrateful by saying this, but when a man becomes 15 or 16 years old he doesn't look at his mother the same way as he looks at his father. And I just think that's something in the makeup of a young man growing up. He's looking at his mom as if she's still kind of soft for him. I don't know how else to explain it, but she's not taking on that stance of a man.

You definitely raised me right, but I think when it came to certain things I just stopped listening. I remember one time you told me that I couldn't go out to this club and once you went upstairs, I just left. I knew there would be consequences when I came home, but I stopped fearing them. Whereas if a father, a male, had told me not to go I just think it might have been different. I think a dad might have threatened to kick me out of the house, telling me that if I wanted to leave I could go ahead and leave for good. You never told me that — you weren't ever going to kick me out and I knew it. I can only imagine how tough it must have been for you sometimes, trying to fill the void that I needed a man to fill. I can't help but wonder how my life, our lives, would have been different if Blaize hadn't died when he did. Yes, I had other men around, but I didn't really pay them any mind because at the end of the day they weren't there full-time. I was craving a level of accountability that I just never really had without a dad.

As a young child I didn't really pay too much attention to the male figure, because you and Gran played that part so well. You were always at my baseball games, at any event that I had as a child. I had your total support in my life. The fact that it wasn't enough in no way reflects on you and your love. I hope you know that I believe you did the best you could with what you had.

I was 15 years old the first time I got caught up with the law. I was riding on an illegal scooter and instead of the police bringing me home, they took me to the station. I remember that you had to come down and pick me up, and I'm sure you'll never forget walking into that precinct and seeing me handcuffed to a chair. I'm sure it broke your heart. As for me, it did scare me straight. But only for a minute.

I remember telling the police that I was more scared of you coming down there to get me than of what I had done. And for about six to eight months, things went back to normal. We started doing things together again — going bowling, watching movies, hanging out watching TV, having my friends come over to the house and hang out. But the pull of the streets was strong.

I stopped making curfew and starting lying to you about where I was, which soon led to me getting into further trouble with the law.

The second time I was arrested, I told you a very convincing story about how the police had wronged me. I know you just wanted to believe me, your only son. And I know you wanted to believe that there was no way that I could have done what the police were accusing me of. So you put out more money. Lost more time at work. Endured more sleepless nights.

• • •

Dear Son,

What was I thinking during this time, as you started to slip away from me so quickly and I tried so desperately to hold on tight? I was thinking that I loved my son. And that I was scared that I was losing you. Nothing else was in my line of vision at this time. Of course the harder I fought, the worse things got. Getting picked up for petty crimes turned into doing time in jail. And when I found out that you were experimenting with drugs, I knew in my heart that this was the beginning of a bad end. I just had no way of knowing at the time how bad things were going to get.

From my perspective, Blaize's death affected you a lot more than your own father's death. I'm not sure whether it was your age or the way he died or a combination of both, but it was right after Blaize's death that I really noticed your behavior start to change. We went to therapy — both individually and as a family — but nothing seemed to help all that much. Looking back, I wish I would have focused more on your behavioral changes and really stayed on you. I thought the counseling I took you to was enough, but there were so many signs telling me otherwise. I should have been more a part of what you were going through and had more open conversations with you. As far as I know, you've never gone to your father's gravesite, but you have been to Blaize's. I have to wonder how your life would have been different if he had lived. I think that you'd maybe be graduating from graduate school by now. I know that he played a complete father role in your life for the short time that he was able. I believe he saw you as his son — no step in front of it at all.

• • •

Dear Mom,

I wonder how our lives would have turned out differently if Blaize hadn't been taken from us so soon.

# 3
## DON'T BLINK

Dear Son,

Your early teen years were a great challenge for me as a single mother. I had such high hopes for your future, but the hardships were many and the obstacles kept coming. Ultimately, I can see now that a lot of the choices you made during this time held you back from your future. I wasn't a mother to give up and I believed that what I had instilled in you in your formative years would lead to a complete recovery in the end, but there were so many difficult days where keeping this faith was more difficult than you can even imagine.

You probably never knew at the time about all the sleepless nights. Midnight, 1 a.m., just listening for that car to pull up, knowing I would remain wide awake until I heard your key in the door. And as time went on, every time I heard a car pass, I'd bolt up, wondering if it was the police coming to deliver bad news.

I don't know if it's any help now, but I wonder if you can trace things back — for your own peace of mind — to see where you zigged when you should have zagged. I wonder if it would be helpful for you to pinpoint exactly when things went so wrong. And I wonder if you really fully comprehend the seriousness of what that road could have been like for you. This thing, which you are now beyond in your life, could have gone in a far worse direction. So many of the guys that you traveled with either are no longer above ground or are never going to come home. I hope that in this reflection you are able to somehow see the substance that was in you that helped you go the distance.

I remember one time when you came home at night and the house you had just left had been raided — I don't think that it was your intent to die or spend the rest of your life in jail, but you did get close more times than I probably even know about. If you had been fully involved in some of the things that happened, I honestly don't know if you'd be alive today. At so many times, you were one bad decision away from death or a lifetime behind bars. I don't blame anyone for the things that you did, but I do know that who and what you surround yourself with matter tremendously. If you hang with good people, you're more likely to do good things. The opposite is also true. And even though it's so easy to say that in hindsight, even though now you hang with people who do what you do, remember that it did take a minute for you to figure all this out after your release.

I know now that you understand that you don't owe anyone anything and I know that you've broken free of the prison mentality and that you understand that everyone at the end of the day has to stand on his own, but I hope that in reflecting on what could have been, about how close you had probably been so many times to traveling down an even worse road than you did, that you remember so that you never go back to that dark place. I believed that I had instilled such good values in you and that somehow things could turn around. I couldn't just speak life into you one time and stop — I said the same thing over and over again because I believed that somewhere along the line it would kick in.

I hear mothers often say that they're tired, that their sons are grown, that they just don't feel like hanging on anymore, and that they're ready to give up the fight. Even though I never gave up on you, I understand the feeling of wanting to. I was so very, very tired. I never knew what was going on in your head, but somewhere along the road I knew that I had to fight the battle against both the addiction to drugs and the behavior that the addiction was causing. It was a hard fight. I think sometimes we stop when things get hard or we think that if someone doesn't give up, it's because they don't have it as bad as we do. But that's just not true. I knew that as long as you were above ground, as long as you were still breathing, I had to keep fighting. I just didn't give myself a choice.

Now I know for sure that every single sleepless night I endured was worth it. It's a fight I would do over again if I had to, even though I pray I never again have to walk down the hard road we traveled together. One of the things that kept me going was my belief that you needed to know that you were worth fighting for — that no matter how many times you chose poorly, turned down the wrong road, or broke my heart, I couldn't give up on you even if I wanted to. I had to find all the goodness in you, bring it to the forefront even on the most difficult of days, and keep telling you that I would fight and never give up. I had to believe that at some point *you* would believe that you were worth saving and that even if I was crazy to keep fighting for you, that I never really had a choice in the matter. That is the depth of a mother's love.

I know now that there was so much right in front of me that I missed. You lost all the important men in your life in such a short period of time and I didn't even fully address it with you like I should have. After Blaize died, I didn't want any other men in my life because every man who had been important to me had died. And yet this didn't take away from the fact that you needed male role models in your life and, at some point, you found what you were looking for on the streets. The men you put faith in had nothing of value to share with you and most of them came from homes much different from what you were used to. But by the time I realized this, you were already gone and the battle was already on — going out in the middle of the night to look for you, going up against mothers who had no control of their households, enduring sleepless nights praying you would come home safe.

It didn't matter where we lived, you were going to find that bad element anywhere. What you found on the streets didn't knock on our door; you had to go on a bus to find it. Our neighborhood was considered Baltimore City, but it was outside of the city-city. When you were able to venture out on your own, you went into a whole different neighborhood that was not so nice. The people you chose to spend time with had no curfews, no leadership, and had been in the world way before you. I make no excuses for you because you had a choice and knew your opportunities were unlimited if you had stayed on track. You chose the difficult path, though, and it took you a long time to realize that everything I said and did came back full circle to haunt you. What I learned through this is that sometimes as parents we have to let go a little and trust that if we have instilled any value into our children then they can make a complete recovery.

• • •

Dear Mom,

My first arrest was like a bad nightmare. I had a friend when I was younger who I used to look up to. I saw him as the big brother I never had. He was a slick dude, always having the latest clothes and coolest new gadgets. And he could play any sport. He also did well in school. In the mid 80's, scooters were really popular in Baltimore City. If you had a scooter you were the shit. And yeah, he had one. He came to my house one evening and I asked him if I could ride it. Of course he said yeah. And as usual, I went overboard and took that scooter on a long joy ride. I was all over the city. Of course I had no license.

I was almost back to the house when the blue lights started to flash. I was so afraid and didn't know what to expect. I pulled the scooter over and from the beginning of the conversation with the officer, I realized that I was in for a lesson. He asked me who the scooter belonged to and even though I answered his questions, I was also being a bit of a smart ass. So he did his job, cuffed me, and took me to the police station. At this point, I was terrified. All I could think about was how you were going to be so mad at me. I wasn't afraid of the situation, but I was terrified of the thought of you having to come down to the station to get me. As usual, you came to my aid to do the motherly thing – save your son. I'll never forget how upset you were when you walked into the station and saw me cuffed. You did all the proper things so that you could take me home. During our ride home was the first real time that you put your hands on me. And I have to admit now that that shit had me at full attention. After that came a conversation filled with love and caring that I think only a mother can give. That was many years ago, but I remember a jewel you dropped on me that day that stuck with me. You told me, "Terrence what you do now in life will follow you always" and of course I had no idea at the time just how true your words were. I have to say that no matter what, through all of my bad decisions and all of my struggles, you always stayed in my corner.

This first incident was just the beginning of my entry into what people called petty crime. Even though I managed to keep things straight for a little while, I did begin having a lot of trouble in school. I couldn't keep my grades up and was barely getting by. If I hadn't had cousin Dink at that time in my life, I would have gotten even more behind than I did.

This was my eighth grade year, which was also the time in my life when I started smoking weed with some of the guys at school. I was looking for my place among the thugs. I think I did that because I was viewed as a well-dressed school boy and all I wanted to do was fit in. The chicks used to like the rough guys in those days. I looked up to this one nigga for real and wanted to be just like him. He came home from Army basic training and had a car. Of course, I thought that was the coolest thing. Anyway, one evening he came to pick me up to go to the mall. I remember that you used to like this guy, so you had no problem with me riding with him. What unfolded that night was just another example of me getting in trouble trying to be someone I wasn't. During the ride to the mall, we stopped to holla at some girls at the side of the road. We didn't know these young women, but that didn't matter to us at the time. It didn't go very well because the girls weren't feeling us. At all. So me being young and stupid, I got out of the car and threw a rock at the girls. I hit one of the girls in the head and not 10 minutes later I was locked up. You came to the rescue once again, and even though you were really upset, we kept this one to ourselves. The only other person who knew was Gran. Speaking of Gran, I miss her so much. But anyway, I went to court for this crime and got a blessing from God because the case was thrown out.

You know, a lot of parents uproot their families out of Baltimore City and move to the County, but I think in some ways it's worse there. There's more money and kids have more unsupervised time. Moving to new locations is not the answer, because bad people are everywhere. The foundation starts in the home and the family and the people you allow in your life. I know we both agree with the fact that it's very important for parents to be careful of who is giving their sons advice. If a criminal is advising your kid, he's gonna be giving criminal advice. If it's a thief, he will be teaching your kid to steal, and if it's a drug dealer, he will teach him how to sell drugs. And on and on. You get the idea.

• • •

Dear Son,

Things really started to change when you were 14 years old. I'd get calls from the school that you were cutting class, not doing your homework, being a clown, not listening to the teachers, and just being generally disruptive. You started hanging out with a crowd I didn't approve of. I told you over and over again that no good was going to come out of the mess — everything that I had warned you was going to happen, in the order it was going to happen, was going to come true. You'd tell me that I didn't even know the guys that you were hanging with. But even though I didn't know many of them personally, I still *knew*. They were grown in a way you weren't. They were exposing you to things that you didn't need to know anything about.

When you started to get into trouble, I punished you in the way I thought was right — took away TV privileges, kept you in the house, and didn't allow you to play baseball. The punishment was effective for short periods of time, but it never seemed to stick. It was like with every day that passed, you became bolder and just started slipping slowly away from me. For a moment I felt like I was failing, like there was something I wasn't doing right, something I wasn't giving you that you needed, something that I was missing. I didn't quite know what to do, but I kept raising you up the best way I knew how. I knew that there was a whole world beyond my front door that I had no control over, but when you walked into our home you still knew how to act right. You'd walk in and know that you needed to take out the trash first thing, even if I wasn't home. Your friends made fun of you for it and called you a punk. They told you that your mama and grandmother were crazy, but I didn't care. If you weren't home at a certain time, Gran and I would roll out and find you — wherever you were — and bring you home. No matter how far you strayed from what you knew was right, the foundation I — and the rest of our family — laid for you was a strong one.

• • •

Dear Mom,

When I was a teenager, maybe 15 or 16 years old, I really started to feel like I wasn't accountable to anyone or anything. I didn't know who I was. Coming up, I was fortunate enough to have everything provided for me that I needed — clothes, toys, everything. And yet once I reached my teenage years something shifted in me, that stuff didn't mean that much to me anymore. I was chasing something else, something much harder to find than the latest pair of kicks. I think that's when things started to really go downhill in my life. I was so up and down with my emotions and my feelings. I would walk into a room and everybody still liked me, but sometimes it would just feel like I wasn't even there. My life became all about running the streets and selling drugs. I started to feel like I couldn't even hold a decent conversation with anyone I loved. Years and years went by that I felt like I wasn't accounted for, like my life didn't matter. Other people may not have thought that, but I felt that way.

I think that no matter how you look at it, growing up without a father is tough. Mom, so much of what you taught me I use to this day – how to be responsible, how to take care of things, how to keep my credit perfect. Now that I'm older, I feel like you did your absolute best to play the parts of a mother *and* father. And yet when I became a rebellious teen, there was a part of me that still knew that you were the one that I could get one over on. I think a lot of boys being raised by women have this mentality – it's like we have this mindset that our mother can pop you around and everything, but she's still your mom. It's the difference between me coming to the house and having to own up to a man or to a mom. I know that the best scenario is having both of them there. I know we both see now the importance of mentoring. We tell single mothers now that they've got to get their sons involved in more activities with positive male mentors, with good men so they don't get pulled in by the bad ones. I don't think I had this mentorship, even though you did everything you could for me. I was involved in sports and other activities, but I don't think it was enough. I don't remember being in any male mentoring program. I wonder what difference, if any, that could have made in my life.

# 4
# UP ALL NIGHT, ASLEEP ALL DAY

Dear Son,

I believe that your imprisonment started long before you stepped into a jail cell for your longest sentence. Once the drugs took hold of your life, your life took a long ride down into a place that's still hard for me to imagine. As with so many drug users, your habit went largely unnoticed by many people close to you. As for me, I knew long before anyone else in the family would believe what was going on. I had to fight my family because they didn't believe there was any way you could be using. You never looked ill or strung out, so it was impossible for them to believe what they could not see. As for me, I knew early on what to look for, so it was harder for me to ignore the signs — no matter how subtle they were.

You never needed the money, but you got into the drug game anyway to make a couple of dollars. I always tell people that you quickly became your own best customer. What I learned from our experience is that if a mother were ever to say that she knows her son is using, then I'd believe the mother. Drug use isn't always visible, but most mothers know their sons in a way that even other close family members don't. For a while, I felt shut out from the rest of our family, a prisoner to your drug use even though I wasn't the one getting high, because I was the only one seeing it and feeling it. It was happening in my own home, and yet nobody would believe that you would ever be one to get caught up in the drug game.

You might wonder when I first began to realize things were going south. Well, I remember when I first found out that you were cutting school and then things just snowballed from there. I started to notice behaviors changing — resisting conversations, being withdrawn, and a changed look that I could only explain by something like using drugs.

I remember how we would leave together in the mornings — when I would go to work and you were supposed to be going to school. Because I had a bit of flexibility in my schedule then, sometimes I would circle back around and reenter the house when you were supposed to be at school. You would hide and I'll never forget the day that I knew you were in the house. I pulled the shower curtain back and there you were, just standing there with nowhere to run. I think that was the day when it really hit me how bad things had gotten. You were probably 17 years old at the time. It started to happen more frequently after that — you were supposed to be at school and I would come home and find you there.

What kept me going was that even though I was losing battles with you every day, I refused to lose the war. I knew that I couldn't give up on you. I couldn't not go on. I knew that if I let myself fall apart, then there was no way we were both going to come out of this mess in one piece. I had to fight through it — and believe me when I tell you that it was a *fight*. Many days, it was like I had to put on a mask just to survive. If I had let the real me show, I would have fallen apart, and that wasn't an option. I really don't know how I got through it — all I knew was that if I didn't, you wouldn't. So I just did what I had to do.

One of the strangest things about this time in our lives is that I don't remember you missing out on a lot of family events. I remember you being there for family parties. You'd still go visit my sister. She'd always give you $10 and swear that you were just fine when we'd talk. For a year or more after I was *sure* you were using, nobody else believed it.

You finally dropped out in 12th grade. Heroin and running the streets became more important to you than most anything including your education. Looking back I wonder what, if anything, I could have done earlier on to point us down a different path than the one we had to travel. I tried not to enable you, although I know that you never wanted for anything and maybe — because of that — didn't learn early on about the true cost and consequences of things. I never let you stay in the house when I went to work, and I didn't co-sign on your behavior. Most of the guys you were selling with had the run of their mother's homes, but it really was never like that with us. You never had the option to just bring people in and out of my house at will. You knew that this was the way things were before you got caught up with drugs and I did stick to my conviction on even the worst of days. I ran our house and so before your brain even got twisted with drugs, you knew the rules. You kind of thought I was crazy and so did your friends, which is exactly what I wanted you all to think.

I was basically on my own through all of this, except for Gran's support. Whatever went down with you, she was my road dog. Even once she knew what was going on with you and all the trouble you were getting into, she never cut you off. She loved you something fierce, even though she did stop enabling your behavior once she really knew the extent of things. I don't think that I could have made it through without her — the court dates, the visits, all of it. It was like all I had to do was pick up the phone, call Gran, and say "Mom, I'm going to go get him down at the station again" and, without even missing a beat, she'd say, "Come pick me up." Your daughter was the other one who never gave up on you, who stood by your side at every turn — including your treatment and incarceration. She'd always remind me to come and pick her up for a visit or a court date. She'd tell you, "Daddy, I just want you to be okay."

I think the thing is that all of us knew that beside the drugs you were a really good person. And yet during that time I really did come to feel like a prisoner in my own home. I'd even lock myself in my own room. Even though to my knowledge you never stole from me or from anyone else in the family, I did still feel like our home had been violated.

• • •

Dear Mom,

My life took a wrong turn when the drugs came in. It started off with weed and yes I enjoyed smoking it with my friends. We would cut school and hang at your house all day. My cousin Dink lived with us during those times. She was and still is my heart. Even though she knew all the same people I did, she managed to stay strong through the peer pressure and came through our teenage years intact.

As I started getting older I had a job as a busboy at a very nice restaurant. I used to love that job because it kept me in nice outfits for school. Even though you always provided me with everything I needed, it felt good to have my own job and be able to do for myself a bit. Sometimes even to this day I do question whether I was given too much as a child. Did you do too much for me because I was your only? I honestly have to say, though, that everything you did was out of love. I can't fault you for any of it because you only wanted the best for me always. And I just took everything that I was given and ran with it. I never really appreciated all that you did for me. I know now that you were just trying to keep the negative world outside our house. I wish that I had really paid attention and listened more to both you and Gran.

The summer before high school was a summer I will never forget. I met my daughter's mother and before I knew it we were caught up and she was pregnant. My daughter Shantell was born when I was only in the ninth grade. I was so scared to be a father and I backed away in the beginning. If I didn't have a strong baby mother I don't know what would have happened to my baby girl, who is such a great part of who I am today. I have a lot of respect and love for DeVonie, my daughter's mother, and if I could change my past, I would have definitely been there for them both more. We are family and I will always be there for Devonie if she ever needs me. My respect for her comes from her never telling Shantell bad things about me, even though if I'm honest there are times when there would have been quite a bit of bad for her to tell. She never played hardball with me when it came to Shantell. She was so young too when we became parents, but she was responsible when it came to our daughter.

So I became a father and didn't have a clue as to what to do. I had to turn to you a lot for help and of course you were there for us. Once again you came to my aid and tried to teach me how to be responsible. Having a daughter at that age was hard, but I tried to adjust and do the right thing. I think for me hearing my daughter say "Daddy" for the first time changed everything. I realized that this was real and this beautiful little girl was mine. And I tried to do right by her, even though I failed so often. By that time, I was already feeling the pull of the streets, hanging with the wrong crowd.

Before I knew it, I had started selling drugs, hanging out, being with different women. I must say I had associates who loved the fact that I had a little girl, like it made me more grown and responsible in some way – even when I wasn't stepping up and being the father I should have been. The guys I hung out with would always ask me about Shantell.

Looking back, it seems like I was always given so many great opportunities to be successful, but I just seemed to make one bad decision after another. And, in the end, that series of bad decisions led me to drugs and ultimately to prison.

I do have to say that having you by my side through everything did give me hope even on the most hopeless of days. Through my battle with drugs I've definitely met all kinds of people. The man I am today has a lot to do with my past life. Having my family there through my irrational thinking showed me that I was somebody. I think if you all had turned your backs on me I would most likely be dead. As I write this, I realize that I am a different man today and I give thanks to God that you and other family believed in me even when I couldn't believe in myself.

One of the worst decisions I made in my life was using drugs. Drugs took my youth and made me do things in my life that I would have turned my back to otherwise. I wanted to be down in the beginning but as things started to progress, it felt like I was drowning. I could see the light above the water, but I just couldn't get there. Or maybe I didn't want to. It's hard to remember.

You tried everything within your power to get me treatment. You went to meetings with me and on your own. You did all you could to support my sobriety, but I just wasn't there yet. I didn't yet want it for myself, I guess. You tried so hard to help me and if I only knew then what I know now, it might have saved us both a lot of heartbreak. You were my angel who never left my side. You were so smart in knowing what I needed, but I just didn't listen. I have to thank you again for never giving up on me. You always knew what I was made of — after all, you raised me right and did a great job of instilling in me everything I needed to be successful.

I know you invested so much money into my treatment. The first place I went to was the Turk House in West Baltimore. I was only 19 years old and was lucky enough that I met a man, Tyrone, who was about 15 years older than me and who took me under his wing and tried to steer me in the right direction. And yet, once I was released from treatment I just went right back to my old ways. Understandably, Tyrone backed away from me and we lost touch until just recently, when I was playing around with your phone and somehow was able to find his number even though we thought we'd lost it. He hung out with us this past year and it was great to see him.

Shantell was about 5 years old at the time and was missing me in a bad way. I remember you telling me that she'd insist that "someone gonna tell me where my father is…" Although at the time I was in a 90-day program that didn't allow visitors. There was no way to explain this to a young child in a way that she would understand, and I'm sad to say that this was only one of many ways that I would deeply disappoint my daughter in the years to come.

I came out of treatment and did pretty well for about 2 or 3 years. But, like most things about my life up to this point, the good times didn't last.

# 5
# HIGHS AND LOWS

Dear Son,

Despite all the highs and lows in the years that followed, I rest easy in the truth that home is your first land of lessons and that you took a solid foundation of love out with you into the world. I have to admit that for a minute I was embarrassed by all that started to go down with you. Like I shared earlier, my family didn't see it right away. I immediately shipped you off to rehab and was so hopeful that that was going to be the one and only time, but as everyone knows by now, that's not how the journey went. I felt positive at first about the possibility of you getting the help that you needed, even in spite of the odds.

There were times when I did think that you used your drug use as a free pass out of jail, knowing that often addicts are moved from jail to rehabilitation facilities. This was such a tumultuous time in our lives. You'd go to rehab, come home and be sober for a week or two. I'd begin to hope that things were going to be different. I'd believe that the nightmare was over. That we were all in the clear again. Honestly, I now see that sometimes you probably got sober just long enough to get me off of your back, to give me some false hope. Before long, we were right back into the cycle again. And so it went.

You continued to get yourself arrested for various crimes and every time I did everything I could to get you out of jail as quickly as possible. I never focused on what you had done, just how I could get you out. You knew that you could always count on me and Gran to make sure you were released as soon as was humanly possible. I would tell Gran, "Ma, I can't do this anymore. He is going to stay this time" and she would always reply, "You can't leave him in there. He doesn't belong there. What do we need to do to get him out?"

So we maxed out our credit cards, put up our houses as collateral, and otherwise jeopardized our own economic stability to spring you time and time again. And before you knew it, you'd be on your way home again. I think that you were so sure that Gran and I would bail you out that you never thought about facing any real jail time.

Eventually, though, the time came when Gran and I could no longer protect you. The judge told you that if you landed in that courtroom again, you'd be doing some time. Well, sure enough it wasn't long before you were caught in a stolen car and sentenced to 18 months.

Those 18 months were hard for me. And lonely. Up until this point, a lot of people hadn't known how much trouble you had really started to get into. I could only make up stories for so long as to where you were and what you were doing. Eventually, I had to start telling people the truth, which was difficult because a lot of people in our lives had known you since you were a baby and still had a picture of you in their minds as that cute little Catholic schoolboy.

As sad as I was when you went away, there was a part of me that was also happy and relieved. In my mind, you couldn't get high in jail. So I knew that you were going to come home clean. And I really believed, and I think Gran did too, that you would have learned a big lesson. You would have learned that we couldn't save you and that going forward you would have to face the consequences of your actions. I thought this would be enough to set you straight. And it was, for a minute.

You came home and things were better for a while. But before long you were back at it again — drugs, crime, and friends occupied your whole life. The next time you were arrested for robbery, I was able to get you out. But before you even went to court, you were arrested again. This time you were facing some major time, but again my mind was still only focused on what I could do to get you out of the trouble you had gotten yourself into.

● ● ●

Dear Mom,

I'm sorry.

# PART II
# DURING

WE MUST ACCEPT FINITE DISAPPOINTMENT,
BUT NEVER LOSE INFINITE HOPE.
– DR. MARTIN LUTHER KING, JR.

# 6

# THE WAITING ROOM

Dear Son,

I couldn't get myself together for that first visit. I don't know if you ever thought about what it might be like to visit your own child in prison. I remember telling Gran, "Ma, I'm not going to be able to do this." And she just told me that I had to. That jail was where you were going to be and that I had to get used to it. Gran and I visited you for the very first time in Jessup Maryland Correctional facility. You were 18 at the time and had gotten 18 months for being in a stolen car. Honestly, I can't believe it took you that long to get some time. You had been in court a lot before that, but you kept getting off.

When I walked into the jail that first time, I couldn't breathe. It felt like my heart just stopped, but I knew I had to go on. I felt so violated, like I had committed the crime. All I can tell you is that having a son in jail is not for the faint of heart. Clink, clink, clink. Just hearing the cells opening and closing is enough to break a mother's heart and spirit. During that first visit, you were still so focused on trying to find a way for me to get you out. You hadn't learned your lesson yet and I remember Gran trying to talk to you about the path you were on. We thought you were listening, but looking back I don't think you really were. It seems that once you were in there you just told us all the things you thought we wanted to hear to make us think that things were going to be different when you came home. My heart hurt knowing the conditions in which you, my only child, were living and from not being able to talk to you and see you whenever I wanted to.

The second visit was a little better than the first and after a while I looked forward to visiting you. If it had not been for my mother, though, I could not have made it through the first time. But I did make it through and even got used to visiting. It became an outing with my best girlfriend. We'd go see you and then hit up the Cracker Barrel and the outlets nearly every weekend. We all found our new normal, not knowing at the time that we were preparing ourselves for not a single 18-month sentence, but the beginning of a long, long road ahead.

I made that journey at least twice a month, lots of times more than that. Each time I went, it was like a weight was lifted off me because sometimes you go back and forth as to why your child is even there and sometimes you question yourself for what you did wrong. After visiting a few times and sitting there talking with you and seeing some slight changes in you, I stopped fearing that when I left you something else would go wrong. A lot of things happen in jail, so many of which I can't even imagine. One thing you can't be in jail is weak — you were the one who had to teach me this. We talked as I visited you and you let me know that I could sleep at night because you were going to do what you needed to do and not initiate anything. And you found a group of guys who were doing the same thing. You taught me you can find a good crew even in prison – for you, they were mostly men older than you who had been in for a long time and kind of looked out for you. It's real easy to get caught up in jail, but somehow you learned to stay out of the line of fire. You learned to really focus, which helped me not worry so much about you. And that was the biggest relief in visiting you and leaving you.

• • •

Dear Mom,

In the beginning, it was like I knew I was away, but I couldn't really accept it. My mindset was that I didn't want to be there, but that I could pretty much be the same person I had been on the streets anyway. So I'd get into a lot of trouble, which caused me to go back and forth on lock up. I remember one particular time when Brandee came to visit me when I was on lock up and she was like, "You're locked up and then locked up in lock up." And she kind of made me look at things differently for the first time.

Brandee really stayed stern the whole time I was gone. She would come and visit and always remind me that I was taking myself away from her and my family because I had created a situation where the glass between us was only the beginning of the many ways in which we were separated from each other. Even though I'm sure she thought I didn't listen to her, I always kept what she said in the back of my mind. I knew she was right, even if I was too prideful to admit it at the time.

I still have the letter that Shantell wrote to me about my being gone. I kept that letter and would look at it often and ask myself if this was really how I wanted to live my life. At that point, I had a lot of years left in my sentence and it was honestly hard for me to get a grip on some stuff. I struggled with seeing how anything that I did behind bars mattered since I was locked up anyway. I would sometimes think, *who cares what I do in here? I've got 7 more years, so I should be able to do whatever I want to survive in the most comfortable way possible.* And yet the constant visits from you, the words of my wife, the letter from my daughter, all of these made me lie down at night and think more deeply about things. You all put things in perspective and made me challenge myself to consider how I would get back on my feet when I got home.

• • •

Dear Son,

I'm glad to hear you say that our visits made a difference, because the whole process of visiting was really intimidating. I remember taking my mother the first time and she was like, "What do they think I have?" as they were searching her. It broke my heart. And then when you get into the waiting room, you realize that almost all of the visitors are moms. We saw very few male visitors in those waiting rooms. Very few dads.

I noticed in my first few visits that a lot of the moms who visited were much younger than me. They were in their mid-30s visiting their 18- or 19-year-old sons. Because of this, I was looked up to as an elder. If these young women came in dressed inappropriately, I'd have shirts in my car to give them. I'd always see the same people week after week. So if some new woman came in and was turned away because she wasn't dressed appropriately, the women would say "Ask Ms. Bettye." A lot of these moms didn't have their own transportation, so they'd catch the bus from downtown Baltimore. And as we know, it ain't no A coach. It got them there, but it could be a 3-hour bus ride. I don't know if the young men always understood the burden they were putting on their young moms.

These young mothers were faithful to be there every visiting day. I wound up knowing the same people because they were always there together. If your son was an even day you were going to know all the even day mothers. I met a mother who lived around the corner from me who I would not have otherwise met, and we started alternating who would drive if I wasn't going with my girlfriend. The waiting room was like a little networking place.

I put a lot of my own hope into these other mothers, which was a lot because sometimes people just look at the cover and don't peel it back. Sometimes we as parents are judged by what our children do. I want it to be real clear that that's a myth. There's no truth in that. One of the things your incarceration taught me is that if you have a friend and you know that her child is incarcerated, you have to learn how to have a gentle conversation with her. Not a "what did he do this time?" accusation, but a conversation to really understand how she and her family are affected. Nine times out of ten you knew this woman from before her son was incarcerated, so why is it any different now?

I have a girlfriend who would tell you that I was there for her in this way. Her son was so lost for so long, and he ended up becoming a police officer. She would tell you that I did right by her son and her because even when her son made a bad decision, I never stopped being her friend. I never judged her or thought less of her as a mother. I learned to never treat other moms like they were criminals too. Even years into your incarceration, I had some friends who only wanted to talk about what you had done over and over again. I remember thinking, *We're already past that. Why are we revisiting that? I don't want to think about what he did. I want to tell you about the progress he's making.*

You know, sometimes I think about what happened to you and I believe it absolutely saved your life. And so when people wanted to talk about you being locked up over and over again, I wanted to move forward. My true friends knew that you were built for greatness and that you had been around greatness, so whatever you did was because you went outside of the box to do it. My mindset got to a place where I knew you did it, you were paying for it, and life needed to go on.

I think you really rediscovered your goodness in there. You didn't learn what you learned inside of there, but you were given the opportunity to use it. For example, once you saw that you could even help one young man, you were all over it. A lot of the guys were 18 and 19 and they were going to come home and needed to be prepared for greatness. I was always proud of you for that.

• • •

Dear Mom,

Before I got locked up, I would always think, *Man, what are you doing to yourself? You need to get yourself together.* But the thing is that I just didn't know how. It took prison for me to find myself again. It took jail for me to sit still long enough to figure it out. I didn't get sober right away. As I said, the first couple years it was like I never left the streets. I was still in the same mindset as being home. That was a part of it too, I think. I realized that I could do what I was doing for the next ten years and go home and still be the same person. But I also knew that if I did that I'd be back with a life sentence. I'd never really get out.

One day a couple of years into my longest sentence I was sitting at a table with a guy I had grown up with. Our stories were similar, but he remembered me before the drugs. And when I shared with him all I had done to get locked up, he just looked at me and was like, "Man, Terrence, I never would have thought you did that, I never would have thought you'd be in here. C'mon man, I know who you are, and this is not who you need to be. Man, this ain't you. You know you're gonna get out and you can't be in here thinking you're gonna be in here forever. This needs to be your last time in here, so you need to work on yourself while you have the chance to be still for a minute." He made me realize that I was in jail and still doing everything wrong. He woke me up. I always kept our conversation in my mind. I didn't stop using that day, but I never stopped thinking about what he said.

As you know, I went through a lot of treatment programs unsuccessfully before I got sober. But I'm gonna be honest with you. Everybody has their own way of getting themselves together, and for me, one day I woke up and said to myself, "Man, that's it." I stopped smoking. Everything stopped and that was something I couldn't believe. All these years I'd been doing this and one day I just woke up and decided I had to be done. And I just started to use all the knowledge I had gained from all of the treatment programs I had been through. I use it to this day. After all the treatments I've been through, I do remember 80% of the information. So as soon as I got sober, the company I hung around instantly improved. I changed my world and then it changed me. For the better.

The crazy thing is that there were a lot more drugs available to me in prison than out here. When you do it in there, it's really because it's right in front of you and there's nothing else to do. So if you want to use, it's so easy to. But like I said above, one day I just got up and was like, *Man. I need to change.* And one day turned into two days, two turned into three, three turned into a week and then all of a sudden it had been six months. And every day during that time I was gradually moving away from guys who were doing drugs in there. It was like, "Hey man, what's going on? Hey, Terrence, what are you doing?" I just ignored those voices and kept it moving forward. I was trying to get away, albeit slowly. I started hanging around with good men who were trying to do right with their lives. It wasn't like I just suddenly stopped hanging out with my old crew one day, but once these guys started to see me moving in a different direction with my life, they backed up off of me and left me pretty much alone.

Six months passed and I had stopped worrying altogether about what those guys thought. I knew I needed to get myself right and be productive, so I wasn't thinking about them or anything else at this point. I was full throttle in getting me right.

# 7
# SETTLING IN

Dear Son,

Anyone reading this might have thought that you would have had enough by now. You did come home for a while and did well. You married Brandee and you all were working toward a nice home. But the thing is that you hadn't really faced up to the real problem yet. The addiction. I do remember that you would go to some meetings, only to find out later that you only went to them so you wouldn't have to hear my mouth.

• • •

Dear Mom,

I'll never forget my and Brandee's wedding day. May 1, 2001 was the date. She was 25 at the time and I was 29. We had a big, beautiful wedding at a country club in Frederick. I know that you hoped that our wedding marked the beginning of a new phase of my life and that all my troubles were behind me this time. I know that you prayed that I would keep a steady job and do what I was supposed to do as a responsible husband and have children and do the right thing. I wanted this too, but that's not how things turned out. It wasn't 6 months after we got married that I was back in jail.

• • •

Dear Son,

By that time, I really had had enough. My health was failing, my money was low, and I was tired. When I found out you were at it again, I knew there was nothing I could do. The hurt was unthinkable and all I wondered was how could this be happening again. You were arrested on a number of charges and I think that was when I finally realized that I couldn't save you. You were going down by yourself. You said you'd never go back again, but I'm not sure if you ever really believed that yourself. I think you were just telling me what I wanted to hear.

I can't believe that only six months after your beautiful wedding you were back in jail, this time for your longest sentence. It was devastating and I'm sure I said a whole bunch of things to you that weren't mother-like, lady-like or otherwise. At that time, I thought that if you had all that in front of you and couldn't do right, then you might never do right. At this point, I was done — no more lawyers or anything. We went to all the court dates and everything, but I stopped pouring money or faith into you for a while.

• • •

Dear Mom,

One of the things I *am* proud of when I think about the time that I was locked up is how I made sure that Brandee was taken care of no matter what. I did have some friends who were good guys who helped us out. If she had a flat tire, I had someone who could take care of it for her. If her furnace went out, she didn't have to worry. Even after she left me and then divorced me, I never stopped loving her or worrying about whether or not she was okay. I understand why she left me. I was a thoughtful and kind person, but drugs made me ugly — which honestly is the effect that I think they have on everyone who uses.

I'm also proud of the way that Brandee and Shantell bonded from the very beginning. Shantell was only 9 when Brandee came into her life and in a family like ours where family is everything, I'm so grateful for their bond.

• • •

Dear Son,

Since we're on the topic of Brandee, I think that her divorcing you during your longest sentence had nothing to do with her lack of love for you. I believe she loved you always, but her pride and some friends got to her, even though I think she realized that even in your absence you were better to her than some of her friends' husbands who were living right in their homes with them.

I guess anyone reading this will probably want to know how you and Brandee met in the first place, since we kind of skipped over all of that. You all met at the BWI airport. She worked in TSA and you worked for Host Marriott Service. You all met when you were going through security on your way to work. That had to have been about 1990 or so. As you told it to me, you talked back and forth for a couple of days and then you took her out on a date and the two of you were together from then on.

The first couple of years you got together I think you were okay.

You did normal stuff that couples do. Brandee grew up in a very good home in a good part of town, so I think that she wouldn't have recognized the signs of a lot of the bad stuff you were getting into because she had never been around it. I do remember when I started noticing signs of your drug use again, I tried to have a conversation with her. She didn't want to have much to do with listening to me and I think she thought that I was just causing confusion and trying to disrupt your household. I do think that she was really the first woman you ever loved because at some point after she broke up with you I remember that you were absolutely devastated.

But like I said, in the beginning I do think things with Brandee were all good, even though you did end up going away for about three years pretty early on in your relationship. I remember when you came home around your 30th birthday you stayed with her family. They never treated you any different. They still don't. I'm so grateful that you have such a wonderful relationship with Brandee's family. I know that her sister had some issues with you during your incarceration, but I don't think she or anyone else in Brandee's family ever stopped loving you.

And some time after you being locked up — probably four or five years in — was when you got divorce papers, which really stopped you in your tracks. I think that was something like you had never experienced before. I don't know if you thought that when you came home you would be with her again, because you still communicated and she still went to visit you, but on paper you all were divorced. I don't know if you thought that when you came home that you would have another chance. Brandee's family was still supportive of you even after the divorce, and her mother still wrote and took all of your calls. The closer the time came for you to come home, though, the more we all wondered what you and Brandee's future was going to entail.

• • •

Dear Mom,

I guess that even on my darkest days I had to find a way to keep some hope alive, but we're getting ahead of ourselves here. You're talking about the time getting closer for me to come home and we haven't even talked about the motion yet.

• • •

Dear Son,

Oh yeah. The motion. There was an instance where you needed to go back to court, but your attorney kept dragging his feet and you never got a court date. So you wrote your own motion to return to court for ineffective counsel. You spent all that time in the library researching how it should be done and the verbiage to use. I guess you knew you had to do it on your own because I wasn't going to pay the $1500 fee again.

You had to do a lot of research to get to the point of finding the right words for the judge to even consider your request. A lot of brainwork had to go into it for the motion to be considered. As you know, most of the young men sitting behind bars are capable of doing a whole lot of amazing things, but they often don't do it because family members enable them. I can't tell you how many times I paid a lawyer for something related to you. That was before I came to my senses.

At first when I told you I wasn't going to pay for the lawyer, you bullied me. But that time I didn't break. You told me that if I got you a lawyer, that you'd be able to do this or that. But I was done with paying for lawyers by that point. There had been a time when I honestly thought that pouring all my money into private lawyers was my only hope of saving you. I depleted my savings and was able to hire lawyers. A lot of people are not so fortunate.

Looking back on it now, I honestly think that as long as mothers are willing to do what I did in terms of paying for lawyers over and over again, then our sons think they can do whatever they want. They hope somewhere that the police didn't cross a "T" or dot an "I" so that their case will get thrown out. These boys are smart and know that their cases could get tossed for a technicality, and so they think that this is their best hope. They absolutely live for it, and I know you probably did for a while too. It does happen, but it's not the best hope. The best hope is to not get in trouble. I've seen mothers use all their bill money just to put down a retainer and keep paying and paying and paying. But from my experience, most young men are going to be offered a plea bargain before they go to court or they'll go to court and get sentenced to whatever the state says they need to be sentenced to. Very rarely do they get off.

Anyway, you did write that motion yourself and were granted a new trial date.

• • •

Dear Mom,

As we both know, you can't just Google how to survive being locked up. There was a lot going on that was really personal that I had to deal with. And there was a lot of stuff I needed help with, like going to court and having people come see me. Even though you didn't have a roadmap, you never stopped showing up. You were there.

In the beginning I was so focused on just trying to get out, until one day I finally realized that I wasn't going to get out until my sentence was over. Every step of the way that I struggled with trying to get out, you were right there struggling beside me. We worked together and I know that we needed to do it together because I had to teach you how to help me. I had to walk you through what needed to be done with the courts, whether that was writing letters, calling parole, or reaching out directly to the prison. I had to let you know how to present the conversation. I knew that you spoke well and that you could handle it from that point. I just don't know what it would have been like without you.

If you don't have any outside help, you're so limited in terms of what you can get done. I know some people think that everything can be done by inmates just writing letters, but sometimes you need that outside help. You need someone to translate things in the outside world, or else it'll just shut its doors on you.

More than anything else, I'm grateful that you never gave up on me. A lot of people say, "I tried," but you knew that you had to *keep* trying. So I don't think we ever gave up, but we did get to a point where we had exhausted every avenue and at some point I was done. I was done fighting.

When I realized that basically all the doors were shut, as far as me trying to get out, I think when I realized that I had done everything I could possibly do, I went up for parole and was denied. I wrote a letter, and the response to the letter was the same thing. I remember that you called the court to see what was going on, but even with the new trial date my hope of getting off on a technicality started to fade.

So at that point, my mind switched because I had already pretty much changed my life, and my mindset, so I just said, "You know what I need to start preparing now because even though I'm not getting out soon, I am going to get out one day." I put a plan together and started to redirect my energy into making my time work for me.

• • •

Dear Son,

I think the good news is that you did get to a place of acceptance where you made a choice to make your time work for you and other men like you. You completed a course in plumbing and earned your Level 2 plumbing certificate. You also started leading workshops with other men to help some of the younger inmates understand what life can be like and to give them hope. You facilitated workshops on life skills, among other topics, as part of the Youth Challenge program and became so excited about sharing your life to help other young men. I was proud of you for starting to tell your story and use it for good. I watched you mature so much in the last years of your sentence. You found a passion for helping others and renewed meaning in your life.

The Youth Challenge program took you into a leadership position where other young men looked up to you, and for good reason. Some of these boys didn't come from the same side of the street as you did, so when you saw that you had something of goodness to share and became a role model in a positive way, then you really just started to soar from there. I don't think you thought you had it in you, but I knew this kind of leadership and heart for service was there all along. I was most proud of how you related to the younger men and how you became someone who was looked up to not for something bad, but for something good.

• • •

Dear Mom,

It felt good to be part of something I believed in. It was one of the first times in my life that I really followed through and completed something and it honestly was the best feeling in the world. The experience taught me that I could give back to so many just by telling my own story. I would teach the younger men that if they were going home with the intention of staying home, then they would maybe have to work at McDonalds to get started. And in teaching this, it changed me. I had to teach them, but also to learn myself that any job that wasn't going to send me back to jail was a good job. I would have never worked in a detail shop or as a security guard before being locked up, not because I was raised with money, but because you did give me all the nicer things in life. I didn't want for anything. But everything I learned in prison taught me how to be humble. I needed to learn these lessons.

The other thing the program taught me was that I had something to offer to others because I saw how I was really helping these guys. And then I realized that if I could help them, I could help myself. The more I told my story to others, the more I began to understand it myself. And the more I saw these guys respecting me for being honest, the more I began to respect myself for telling the truth. I never stood up and told them I was this big drug dealer guy who came from a home where we struggled to keep the lights on. That wasn't my story. So I told them that I was just a regular guy who made some really bad choices and how I struggled with addiction along the way. And I think it was during this time that I really started to think about coming home and what it was going to take to put my life in order. I started to put together a little plan for myself so that I wouldn't stagnate. When I got to prison, I didn't see how starting at the very bottom could get you to the top, but as my mind began to change, a whole new world of what was possible opened up to me.

• • •

Dear Son,

It was around that time that I began to look forward to you coming home. I began to see that you were going to have choices in your life. Hearing you make plans for your time and then carrying out those plans gave me hope. One of the things I used to always tell you is that you had to make use of what was available to you, and you did that so well.

# 8
# THE CARDS

Dear Son,

Every weekend I'd go to the card outlet and buy a group of greeting cards. They were just like the ones you'd get from Hallmark, but a lot cheaper — four cards for a dollar. When I'd pick them out, I would always think about a particular idea that I might want to get across to you. Some were thinking of you cards, some were words of encouragement that I liked, and some were funny ones that I could send along with a money order.

Then, on Sunday, I'd write out all the cards for you for the coming week. Often, I'd base the cards on what our last week had been like and what messages or words I thought you might need to hear most. I'd address all the envelopes and number them and then put one in the mail every single day.

I think the time when I started sending you these daily cards marked a turning point in how I handled your incarceration. I stopped catering to your every wish and started to think about what you really *needed* to survive in there. I don't think you were alone in the way you tried me. I think this happens with a lot of young men and their mothers during lock up. It's as if young men know their mothers feel guilt, and that if we miss a step or don't do something you ask of us we'll feel even more guilt. When you first went in, I didn't quite know what to do with myself. It had just been you and me for almost all your life — so it was a huge void knowing that I wasn't going to see you every day. You weren't there to take out the trash, celebrate important times with your family, or watch your daughter grow. And I think I just didn't know what to do except to channel all the emptiness I was feeling into doing everything and anything you asked of me.

I had to unravel this as a parent. It's easy for you to say now that I did everything right, but there were so many times during your incarceration that I questioned myself. I wasted so much energy wondering what I couda, woulda, shoulda done.

So I had to work on changing my mindset and the cards were a part of that. I believed in the importance of having communication from home to jail. My thought process was that as long as you were still being updated as to what was going on with the family, you would have hope that when you did come home you'd be able to pick up with us and move forward. People would ask about you in a loving way and the cards gave me the opportunity to share this light with you.

One of the things that broke my heart was when I would hear other inmates say, "Nobody visits me, they're sick of me, they're tired of me." I always wanted you to know that even though you had hit a bump, you still had a home and a family that loved you. And I believe that's the main reason that you had hope — knowing that when you came home everyone was still going to love you, they wouldn't be hiding their pocketbooks or looking at you sideways. So I think that gave you hope and helped build you up to the man you are today.

On the journey we took with you through your incarceration, it was important to me that we didn't let time stagnate. I wanted you to know what was going on with me and our family so that when you came home it wouldn't be awkward. You always had that pipeline to what was going on at home. I loved how you sent cards back to us, too. I remember that on Christmas we'd all get special, homemade cards from you that were way better than Hallmark. I also remember the year that you had little pillows made for us. You were always having personalized crafts made to send home to us.

I always had to remind myself that you didn't kill anybody or make another family cry. I can't even imagine how hard you would have gotten if you hadn't felt any love from your family.

I guess at the end of the day, I just wanted to make sure that you came home whole, not broken. I hate to think it, but as I look back I really believe that the timing of what happened to you was the right time. It was time for you to be off the streets. I think the only other option for you would have been death. Your sentence brought a calmness and consistency to our world. No more ups. No more downs.

• • •

Dear Mom,

Those daily cards gave me life. I don't know what else to say about them except thank you. They were a constant for me in a time when I was afraid that I would lose, had already lost, everything. You know, when Brandee left me I think that both hurt and helped me. I want people to know that even though she divorced me, she never really left me all the way because we did still communicate. Without her, I think I did get stronger and kind of pushed myself to be better because I wanted to grow into the man that she deserved. I was in the absolute worst place in my life when she left me. Even though I was a good person at heart, I had done a lot of bad things and caused her a lot of hurt. I think I knew that Brandee had to leave me in the same way that I knew you had to stick by me. I knew you weren't going anywhere, and those cards every single day reminded me of that.

# 9
# THE PROMISE

Dear Son,

Well it's been almost four years since Gran died and I know how much it hurt you to be away in her final months. Nobody had a grandmother like Gran. She was the apple of your eye. I don't think you even loved me as much as you loved Gran. She would always, always encourage you to do the right thing, telling me, "Well, that ain't the worst he could do." That was one of her favorite lines.

You were raised under her almost all your life. When you weren't locked up, you would always be sure to go and check on her, no matter what you were going through. The two of you would sit and talk, and I remember her telling you that all she wanted you to do before she closed her eyes was to do the right thing. If she could see you right now, I know that her chest would be sitting right out because everything that she ever taught you about what it looks like to do the right thing, you're doing that now.

As you know, one thing she pounded into our lives was "education,

education, education." We're talking about a woman in her 70s getting her GED. Not only did she do that, she used to tutor the students at Baltimore City College in Algebra. We don't know how she knew the subject. All the young people used to study with her. She was so smart. She got her AA from St. Mary's College in Food Handling and Sanitation. She had never worked before, but in 1986, when she was in her 70s, she got her first job. She went on to be a site manager for Baltimore City's Eating Together program.

Most of the people she serviced were senior citizens — we used to always joke with her, "Ma, you realize you're a senior citizen right along with them," and she would say, "Yeah, but they old." She raised us, and then our kids and everybody else's kids.

Her focus on education was powerful because most of the young people in our family have at least a decent level of education. We have a lot of college graduates in our family and the ones who didn't go to college have a lot of stability in their jobs, staying 20+ years like I did in the same career. I can hear Gran's voice telling me, "Oh, you're going to start all over again? What if you don't like them too. Girl, you're gonna stay where you at. Unless you're going to own your own business, it's not going to be much better." And that led me and my two sisters to stay 20+ years in the same places, elevating ourselves to higher levels within our companies.

I think that kids have to *see* that kind of dedication. I used to hear Shantell say "I'm sick of this place. I'm about to find me another job." Stability in the household is really, really important. I was able to tell you, "Son, you need to stay where you are unless something better becomes an opportunity for you" because that's what Gran taught me. And when I said that to you, I know that you knew I was telling the truth because every day I was going to get up and head to work at the Holiday Inn.

• • •

Dear Mom,

I have every letter Gran ever wrote me from every time I was incarcerated. She was everything to me. She never gave up on me. I did get to see her one month before she died. In court. And she had one more chance to tell me to do the right thing. I made a promise to her that day that that was going to be the last time I'd ever put myself and my family in that position. That that was the final time. And that's a promise I intend to take with me to my grave.

At the end of the day, your and Gran's love have meant everything to me. Your love was pure. You were the backbone through my entire incarceration. If you hadn't stuck with me, I don't know what would have happened. I can't even imagine how hard it was for you some days. I understand why mothers give up on their kids and I don't think that any mom should have to take abuse from anyone, even from her own kid. But I think that you being there always helped me to get to where I am right now. If you hadn't of shown me that type of love I don't know what would've been. Sometimes I used to think, *Damn, these women are like 60 and 80 years old and keep driving up these mountains themselves. If they can show me this kind of love, then I need to get it together.*

You endured because you loved me. You and Gran taught me what it means to never, ever, ever give up.

• • •

Dear Son,

I know that a lot of people talk about making peace with loved ones before they die, but I don't think you had to make any peace with Gran because the one thing that Gran always knew was that she had helped raise you right and that she had always done right by you. I feel the same way about you and me. I could go tomorrow and I would know that I did right by you.

# PART III
# AFTER

ME AND YOU, WE GOT MORE YESTERDAY THAN ANYBODY.
WE NEED SOME KIND OF TOMORROW.
— TONI MORRISON

# 10
## FREEDOM

Dear Son,

I'll never forget the day of your release. You had planned for a friend of yours to go out and pick you up, so I didn't go. It was really exciting, though, to think about what it was going to be like – me, your aunt, my best friend, Brandee, and some other family members planned a big soul food homecoming for you. We wanted you to know that, above all else, you were coming home to a place where you were loved without condition.

As for any people I felt might bring some negative energy to your reentering, I removed them from my life before you were released. There were some people I had to remove – some who only wanted to keep the conversation going about you being in jail. And then there were some who weren't going to look at you any other way except as a criminal. I just knew that you needed supportive, loving people around you and that it was my job as your mother to set the example for what your life was supposed to look like. I thought that if I could do it, it would be easier for you to remove these types of people from your life, too.

None of us could have known for sure that you were going to do so well upon your release, but I had seen you take baby steps and had seen your patience as a sign of maturity and growth above all else, so I was very hopeful.

• • •

Dear Mom,

Once I walked out the door, I knew that I was free forever. Free to build my life, free to right all of my wrongs.

You know, someone asked me just the other day what freedom meant to me. And it got me thinking. It's weird I'm going to say this, but freedom is me getting out of my bed and getting myself a cold drink of water when I want it. Those ten years took everything from me. I remember Gran used to say, "Man, you're not gonna be able to get you something cold to drink if you keep doing this." I said "What?" She said, "If you keep doing this, you're gonna get yourself locked up and you can't get yourself a cold drink or soda." I never understood what that really meant. Until I did. In jail, we were on the clock for everything. Somebody is always telling you what to do. I've been home for four years and certain things I do truly let me know that I'm free.

As you know, I work early mornings now and sometimes Brandee asks me why I jump out of bed so quickly. Sometimes I have to work at 3 in the morning, so I wake up at 1:30, and I might go to sleep with the baby at 10 and jump right back up and that's freedom to me. I know I'm free, and a lot of times this is what makes me happy getting up.

## FREEDOM

And freedom to me is going to get my daughter and taking her to do what she wants and taking her to swim class. When I get up on Sunday mornings and take her to swim class, I know that I'm free. The whole time in there I might be smiling to myself, *I'm free, I'm here with her.* That's freedom to me.

It wasn't just being locked up behind bars that imprisoned me. I was locked up within myself. So me being able to get up in the morning and not think about addiction is freedom. To sit down and write this is freedom. Sometimes I just sit in my own world and when people ask me what am I thinking about, I tell them that I'm just sitting there enjoying the moment and being free.

# 11

# RE-ENTRY

Dear Son,

While you were gone, your room became your granddaughter's and daughter's room for a while, so I fixed up my basement for you. I had the bathroom redone completely and made the space comfortable and cozy, like an apartment. I made it like it was all yours. I didn't want you to come back and think that you didn't have a place to call home. I wanted you to come home and feel home. So I took the time to prepare it especially for you. I didn't want to be one of those moms who said, "Well, you can get a blanket and pillow and sleep over there." I made a prepared place for you because I wanted you to feel like you could stay here for as long as you wanted or needed to. You and Brandee had a home, but you needed a minute to just breathe and get yourself together without all the responsibilities of the world weighing down on you. You needed a minute to figure out what you had to do.

I had researched a couple of programs for you, and then I backed off and kind of let you figure it out. I felt like at some point you needed to go solo. One of my biggest weaknesses is seeing a need before it arises, but I'm learning to back off — and you'll tell me now that you'll figure it out and then let me know if you need something. Above all else, this lets me know that your thought process has matured and I'm just really excited about that. My biggest challenge during this time was just learning how to step back — if you needed me, you always knew that you could come and ask me. It was time for me to let go and let you take your life in your own hands, because part of the issue had been that I had always tried to run everything.

I do have to say, though, that it was really nice having you here for a time. You were very respectful of my home, helping to keep it really clean and never letting anything get out of place.

• • •

Dear Mom,

When I was released in August of 2012, I'm grateful that I had a place to come home to. The first couple of weeks I spent all my time putting my life on the outside right — getting my license back, looking into programs, signing up for some classes, getting a part-time job as a bouncer, working odd jobs, getting certified as a detailer, getting a car. It took me about 18 months of waiting and working patiently, just focusing on making ends meet, until I landed the job that I now have.

I think a lot of young men and their families don't know that there are so many programs now to help young men with records reenter society and be okay. Many of these programs are free and can help prepare you for a trade that can lead you to a successful career. The old excuse of "I can't get a job" really isn't the issue anymore. You just have to be willing to invest the time into yourself and not hide behind an old, outdated excuse. I researched a lot of these programs while I was still in prison so that upon my release I'd have a bit of a jump start in getting my life back together.

I'm also grateful that you let Brandee stay with me most of the time at your house in those first months. I really did need some time to just sit back and reflect before I came up with my game plan. Before I could drive, I knew I didn't want to bother you with taking me around everywhere. That's why I prioritized getting my bus pass and then permit and license as soon as possible. Within a month after my release I had all my business taken care of, which just proves what you can do with a little bit of focus and some support.

When I first came home people just watched me to see what I was going to do and which moves I was going to make. One of the stereotypes surrounding Black men and incarceration in this country — that all Black men end up in jail — is one that I had fallen right into. But when I was away I woke up and realized that so much of the way I thought needed to change if I was going to make it on the outside. It woke me up. I realized that I was going to have to do some stuff — like working at McDonalds or washing cars — that was just not in my story before. Before I would have preferred to take an easier route to get some money, but once I started doing right and earning checks, I realized that it wasn't that bad.

I hope anyone reading our story sees that if a man can come home and set his mind to say that he is going to try this thing the right way, then anything is possible. I remember Gran would always say, "Just try. Keep going. If you keep working, things are going to get better." And you know what? That's exactly what happened. I kept getting better and better jobs and people helped me more once they saw that I was on track. I knew that my desire not to go back to that world had to be stronger than any temptation. I had to tell myself that I never wanted to be incarcerated again and have people dictate my every move. I'm too old to have somebody tell me when to eat and drink, when I can sleep and when I can wake up. So I think sometimes looking back and remembering what I came through helps me to keep moving forward.

I do feel that I've overcome a big obstacle in getting where I am in my life because a lot of people just write you off when you do that kind of time I have. Luckily, I had a good family who stood by me and wanted to see me do well. I know that that keeps me going now and allows me to appreciate everything I have. I know that in some ways the fact that I'm even alive is a miracle. So for me to be here now and actually be successful and able to do things with my family and not have to live paycheck to paycheck is wonderful. The things I'm doing now are the same things I used to avoid because I didn't ever want a struggle. I wanted everything now, now, now.

When Gran died while I was still locked up, I think I began to see that I had to figure out how to take care of myself. You would have done everything for me, and you did. When I was locked up, you kept everything in order for you, for me. And I knew that I didn't want that any more. I didn't want anybody to have that much control over me. I wanted to get on my feet on my own. So I started cutting the cord slowly. You did everything for me when I was away and I wanted to get to a place where I could be the one in the position to do for you. I didn't want to use you as a crutch when I got home. When I was gone, I needed you to do for me because I was so limited in what I could do for myself. But once I came home I needed to learn how to take the limits off my mind and figure out how to make it on my own.

I remember when I first came home you had a list for me — go to this program, go here, do this, do that. And one day I had to tell you that I needed to do it on my own. I knew that as long as I stayed on the right side of the law, that I was going to be okay. I had to find out on my own what my niche was. And I figured it out. I worked at a car wash and I worked as a bouncer. One thing led to another until I finally got the job I have now. I learned to never let go of the fact that I was working for a dollar. This kept my mind absolutely in the right perspective — that you work for a dollar and you do whatever you are asked to do. I kept telling myself, *It's gonna get better, it's gonna get better, it's gonna get better.* I didn't let that thought go. And it did get better. Every step was a better step.

• • •

Dear Son,

I see it clearly now, the ways in which my support lifted you up and the ways in which it kept you down.

• • •

Dear Mom,

I know my story, our story, is a good story, because I've watched hundreds of guys like me who still have my old mentality. And a lot of them now see me being home and see me where I am and they're like, "Man, if Terrence is doing what he's doing and going where he's going, it can't be that hard."

When people ask me how I've done it, I have to say that working on my own attitude and beliefs has been the most important thing. Because you still have thoughts of the old life and the drugs. If somebody tells you that those thoughts go away, I think they're lying because that bad side never goes away. You just have to focus on what you're doing and be happy with what you have. I think about that every day, every week, and about what will happen if I do anything wrong — whether it be selling drugs, using drugs, or anything I know is going to put me on a bad path. It wasn't just me using drugs. I sold them and made a lot of money for a long time doing it, so I definitely have to look at that and know that's not success. That's why I say people have to get a mindset of appreciating what you have. And I think when you're working for it, you appreciate it more. So I have less now, but I have more. I appreciate all that I have right now. And I know that I'm going to have everything I want if I just keep working. I may not have it all tomorrow, but it's coming my way.

I had to struggle. I had to learn patience in prison because I didn't have any before. Just being locked up taught me a lot of patience and taught me that I was nothing special. I was one of 2,000 other people who, in the eyes of the system, was just another number. I learned humility in there. And every year that I wanted to get out and I knew I couldn't, I had to sit back and figure out how I was going to do the rest of the time. How I was going to survive. And I did figure it out.

I hope that any young man reading our story sees that you just have to keep going and eventually life is going to get better. If you hit one thing and that doesn't work, you just have to try a different route. For example, I almost gave up on getting my CDL license recently because I kept failing the test. And one of the guys I work for was like, "What you giving up for? Every time you take the test you get one more answer right, so eventually you're going to get them all right." And that's what happened. I failed three times and then went down there and passed. So it's important for guys to understand that if you just keep going, you'll get there.

Back when I was washing cars, that same guy had been watching me and one day he told me to put in an application at the trucking company. I didn't go for a week because I was comfortable doing what I was doing, and he kept saying, "Come on! It'll change your life." Finally, I put in my application and the company must have liked me, because I got the job. Getting the job changed my life because I never imagined that I could have my CDL. I finally had a career to call my own. Now I believe that life will only get better from here. Opportunities continue to come my way and doors keep opening up. I make sure there's always another door I can go through to keep me going.

I'm still on parole, and when I go to see my probation officer and I see guys who feel the same way I used to, thinking they can never get a job. And I have to tell them now, "Look! You just can't give up. That job says no? Then go somewhere else. You can't say what you're going to do and not going to do. Like don't say that you're too good to work at McDonalds or wash dishes." I had a buddy who said that he had a job going door to door selling something and they were paying him wages and he said that he wasn't doing that anymore. And I told him that he just didn't want to work then. For me, every job I took got better than the last one. I would work ahead and another guy would see me and say, "Hey I'm hiring at my place," and it would get better and better as I went along. But if you just close the door on everything then you never know if you're able to get ahead.

At the end of the day, I know that I'm still going to have doors shut in my face and that's okay. One of the biggest things I had to realize was that no one had done this to me. I had done it to myself. I had to endure some of those doors being shut and companies not wanting to hire people coming home from jail. But if you keep at it, doors will start to open. You've got to keep going. I've got to keep going.

And I've got to stay sober. I know that I can't avoid everybody. I go to the store and see the same guys I ran with. But seeing makes me stronger because it reminds me of the place I never want to return to in my life. Just the other day I was getting into the car with my daughter in front of your house when I saw a guy I went to high school with. He's still doing the same thing. We used to run together. And when I looked at him, all I could think was, *thank God for my life*. So I can't avoid it all, but I think it makes me stronger because I don't want to be that person anymore. I use all the tools I've learned about being sober every day. I don't put myself in certain positions, even if sometimes my mind goes to a dark place. It's an addiction and so I have to remind myself of the "what ifs" on days that are hard. And my strongest "what if" is what if everything you worked for would be gone? It snaps me right back into reality. This is something I work on with my wife, I do this every day.

But the biggest part that helped me when I got out is that everybody knew about my drug addiction. I didn't make it a secret. Even if they had had a thought that I was using before, they knew for sure when I got out. I realized that being honest opened up a whole world of support to me. See, back then a lot of people didn't know, so if I got clean for a minute and felt like

I wanted to use again, there were only certain people I could call up. Now I can call up anyone. And that's another tool I use. I haven't really felt that way since I've been home, but if I ever did feel that way I could call anybody — Brandee, her mother, you. I didn't even realize how much my secret had me in a box. I couldn't get any help for real. So when I was in jail, I opened up to everybody, except one person. Gran. She died before I could ever tell her from my own mouth.

So being open helps me out. From time to time, close friends of mine will be like "You alright? How you feeling?" I didn't go to formal recovery meetings, but I know the steps and I have support. I have guys I work with who have been in the same situation and we talk about it all the time — how our lives were and how they are now. We have our own meetings. Every day we talk and share how thankful we are to be where we are and how we are grateful in our own way for being successful. None of us ever thought we would be doing the stuff we're doing and so we celebrate that.

For example, I never thought I would be able to make more money than Brandee, who has a college degree. I always thought that, even when we got back together, she would be the one making more money. But now I'm able to take care of the majority of the bills, and the guys and I talk about this kind of stuff. It's always a grateful conversation. We remember where we were. There's a guy who I work with now who was locked up with me. He slept next door to me. We talk like 20 times a day now. It helps keep my mind right because we had the same path, so our conversations are like a recovery meeting every day. Knowing that we share a similar path, we specifically talk about drugs, where we've been, and where we never want to go back to. That's what keeps me strong now.

Honestly, there was a long time when I just never thought I was going to stop using. I used to hear that people were clean for years and I was like, *Man, that's never gonna happen. That's never gonna be me.* But now I understand. Now I see that that is me. It's almost 10 years that I have been clean.

And once I came home, because of my lifestyle with drugs and addiction, I had to prove to people that I was going to do something different. I know that people say you don't have to prove anything to anybody, but I knew that I did have to. For all those years I didn't do right, and so I had to prove that I wasn't going to be living the way that I used to live. I had to prove to myself first, and then to you and all the other people I loved, that I could live right and do right by you all. And I have.

# 12

## FAMILY MAN

Dear Son,

You came home in August of 2012 and remarried Brandee in October of 2013. I saw it coming because when you came home, she was here. She was at my house and she never left. I let the two of you stay at my house, because I thought it was a good idea based on the circumstances of you not being married. I wanted you to be here with no interruptions. When you left my house, you left together.

Your second wedding was even more beautiful than the first. It was held at the beautiful home of a dear family friend in Serverna Park. Having your granddaughter participate in the wedding was something special.

Your second daughter, Alayah, was born on April 19, 2014. You are an amazing father. When Alayah was only two weeks old, you were already taking her out by yourself, diaper bag and everything. She's been your road dog ever since. All day long when I'm watching her, she gives me the phone and says, "Here.

Call Daddy." You cook, clean, and take care of your baby. By the time Brandee gets home from work, Alayah has eaten and had her bath. You and Brandee are such a good team. You each have your chores and then you have the things you do together. I don't see that much, so I do think your relationship is special. I'm proud of you for the great relationships with all four of the ladies you have in your life — your two daughters, your wife, and your granddaughter. They are all treated well, they really are.

As of February 8, 2016, you are the proud owner of your CDL license. The job you have now is a job you never thought you could get because of your record, but you never gave up the dream. You found it and claimed it. You always wanted to drive trucks and that's what you are doing now. All things are possible.

I don't know if you ever thought that life could be this good, based on the things you did in the past. But I hope that if your journey, our journey, teaches people anything it's that there is a life after the past. You say often that you wouldn't change a thing, because everything you have in your life now is what you've worked hard for.

I'm most proud of you because of the family man you've become. Even though your own father wasn't in your life long enough for you to learn what a real father is, I think that you learned enough from your grandfather and Blaize and the other men in your life about what it means to take care of a family. You especially know how to treat the women in your life right. I spent a lot of time with you teaching you about respecting everyone, especially women. And so it's nothing but a joy to watch you with your own family now.

• • •

Dear Mom,

I'm so proud of my family now, but I'm not perfect. I think that when it comes to Shantell, we still have a long road ahead of us. It was a lot of years, a lot of hurt, and that kind of healing isn't going to just happen overnight. I try to be there for her, but I missed a lot of time in her life. I know she loves me, I'm her dad, and I know she knows I love her, but my time in jail really took a toll on her. But I can't turn the time back, so I know I just have to be there for her from this moment on.

Since I've been home, I've been with her every step of the way. Even if she wasn't there. I mean, we have our times where we fall out and go weeks without talking. And when this happens I pick the phone up and call her and say, "Alright. It's been long enough." I know I have to be the one to pick up the phone because her mindset is that she knows how to do it without me. I mean, I was gone for 10 years, so she can go without talking to me. So I pick up the phone and call her. I tell her, "Alright. That's it. I'm gonna see you such and such day. It's over." We move on. That's the bond we have. And I'm her father, so I'm going to tell her what she needs when no one else is going to tell her.

Even when I was away, she would ask you to tell me to call her when she needed something. So, that part of our relationship has always been like that because she knows I'm gonna give it to her straight, even now that she's grown and has her own family. I say what I want to say because I lost a lot of years with her, so I like to be there for her a little more now that I can.

I feel bad because sometimes she'll be around and see her little sister and I wonder if she feels a certain kind of way — like I never took *her* to swim class — even though she's grown. It must be hurtful, so I try to still do for her even though she's an adult. I come to her and make her a part of whatever is going on. I don't know how to really say all this. It makes me a little sad. Because I don't like her to see all that she missed out on, all she should have gotten, but didn't. I know there were a lot of things that happened to Shantell when I was away that probably wouldn't have happened if I had been here. So we had a lot of issues that took a big toll on our relationship. She's comfortable with me, but I don't think she'll ever get over it. How could she?

Having had my struggles and being a Black man in America today, I feel like I need to hold myself accountable for all of my actions. I need to be a good father and supporter and I need to give back more to you and my family than what I took away. More than anything in life, I want to be a good father. I focus a lot of my energy now on taking care of my younger daughter and this gives me hope.

Brandee asks me how I do it — how I get up early and get on the road six days a week as a truck driver. And all I can say is that now my life is driven by a different purpose. I used to just focus on how it felt like I could never get ahead, but now that I have accomplished a few things I see that so much of how I saw things was just in my head. I put that wall up to say that I couldn't be successful because I had a different definition of success. I used to think that success was only about getting a college degree, and then when I got older, I thought I'd find success in the hustle. But now I define success as feeling comfortable with the arena I'm in — having a good job, going to work, being able to take care of a home. I don't worry anymore about how I'm going to take care of this, how I'm going to do that. For years I felt like I never had enough and never was enough, but now I just tell myself that I have enough and that I am grateful for it all.

As a Black man I think the most important thing right now is taking care of my younger daughter. She deserves so much. I watch other fathers who parent how I did with Shantell and then I look at myself now and say, *Man, you're doing good. You're doing what you're supposed to do.* There was a time in my life when I didn't think I stood for anything, and now I know that I stand for my family.

You know, looking back there were so many times when I was in the midst of running the streets and you would tell me, "Terrence, you may have a lot of money, but you're still doing bad." I used to tell you that I understood, but I didn't understand. Then down the road I realized that as long as I was doing and selling drugs, I could have a million dollars but at the end of the day I wasn't living right. What I'm doing now is pure. There are no interruptions in my life. It's pure living. Paying my bills, having a little bit of coin to do what I want to do, taking care of my family — I wouldn't trade my life now for anything in the world.

So taking care of my family, and especially my younger daughter, that's success to me. As a mom, I know you always want to say good things about your son. And yet for a lot of years, you didn't have much good to say. I mean, everybody knew I was a good person under the mess, but how many times are you going to share that? Today, people know about the stuff I've done, but now you really have a chance to talk about your son with pride.

• • •

Dear Son,

You know I've always loved you, but now that love radiates

with pride. Loving you and my granddaughters and great-grandchildren is the greatest joy of my life. I can't imagine anything better than this.

# LESSONS

## BETTYE BLAIZE

### FOR MOTHERS

1. Your son is not grown at 13 and is not the man of the house, regardless of whether there's a man at home or not. That's too much responsibility for a boy, and when we give our boys too much responsibility at an early age it often leads them into a life of grown man's stuff before they are ready.

2. Be careful who you expose your children to, especially if you're single and dating. Your son doesn't need to date everyone that you do. Even when it's not convenient, make sure that before you bring someone into your home and around your children you really know that person.

3. Lead by example. Teach your babies how you want them to treat you. Yesterday, I saw a boy with his mother and his underwear was hanging out. He was with his mother. We can do better than this.

4. Address trauma with your son when it happens, even if you yourself are grieving. Seek resources and get help when you need it. Talk about death, even when you don't know exactly what to say or how to say it. Often, the worst thing we can do

is say nothing. Do not underestimate the effect that tragedy has on your son, even when he doesn't know how to express that grief.

5. If your son does not have a strong male role model in his life, you need to bring a sober, responsible man in as early as possible. It doesn't have to be a relative – it can be a neighbor, a college kid down the road, or someone from church. Raising sons is a hard job for mothers and society says that a mother can't teach a boy to be a man. I don't agree with this entirely, because even though we can't teach our sons everything, we can teach them a lot about being gentlemen. We can teach them how to open doors and pull out chairs. But then we need that man who can walk them into manhood. It's up to you to seek out a person who you feel is a good fit for your son and who can teach him and help him learn.

6. Learn how to ask for help when you need it. As mothers, grandmothers, and aunties, we should be teaching our boys that asking for help is not a sign of weakness.

7. Take ownership of your son's living quarters. The only way you're going to find anything like drugs, alcohol, or weapons is if you look. I hear some mothers say, "I don't feel right going to his room looking through his stuff." Terrence knew I'd enter his room, flip a mattress, dump the trash can, or look through his drawers in a heartbeat. It's your home and when your son tells you that it's "his room," let him know that in fact it's your room in your home and you're just letting him stay there.

8. Whatever harm's way your son might put himself in while in your house is also going to put your entire family in harm's way. If he has drugs in his room and the police stage a raid,

your entire family may go to jail. Be mindful of this as further justification as to why #7 is important.

9. If your son comes into the house with a $200 pair of shoes on and you're struggling to pay the household bills, then you probably need to have a conversation with your son as to who is buying those shoes for him. Chances are, if someone is buying your son expensive shoes, that person is going to become his "friend," and this "friend" might just be the one who puts the first 8-ball in his hand.

10. Be very vigilant of any change in behavior, no matter how small it may seem. Any behaviors that surface need to be addressed at the time. Do not wait, do not excuse the behaviors away. Address them.

11. Understand that if your son is using, he will do things that he would never do sober. He will lie, steal, and do all sorts of other things that might have been unimaginable to you before. What you're looking at is not necessarily what it seems – just because someone looks "fine" doesn't mean that he is fine. Do not be fooled – if you see any reoccurrence of behavior, even in another form, you need to acknowledge what you're seeing immediately. It might not stop the behavior, but it lets him know that you are aware.

12. Everyone who is going to be involved in the recovery needs to know about the addiction and understand. When your son comes home, he's going to be clean, so everybody needs to be educated so that you can create environments that support recovery and don't fuel addiction.

13. When visiting your son, it's not a good idea to talk about why he's there. It really is not a big issue – you both know why he's

there. He probably would much rather spend the time talking about how things are at home and how things are going to be in the future. Tell him about yourself, what's going on with you. You want to make what has already happened a thing of the past. Once he left court and knew what his charges were, there's really nothing new to talk about there. Everyone knows his charge and every day he's there he has all day long to think about the whys. Keep the conversation focused on other things.

14. Don't make your problems his problems.

15. Unless you're not home, please take your son's calls. Set guidelines with him if the calls present a financial hardship for you. Communicate clearly about when he can call and how often you can accept his calls.

16. Words of encouragement in the form of cards or letters are going to make him look forward to coming home and let him know that there's someone waiting for him to come home to. Be consistent in your communication to your son.

17. Be consistent in your visits. If you say you're going to show up, show up. If you can't make visits on a consistent basis, find others in the family — a favorite cousin, a sibling, an aunt, a grandparent — who can take on this responsibility of visiting. Coach these visitors to say something along the lines of, "I asked your mother could I come and visit you instead of her today." The important point is that your son knows that he is loved and that there are people to stand in the gap.

18. Respect other loved one's desires to visit as well. If someone requests to go see your son without you present, respect that

request. Make it clear, though, that if they commit to going in your place they need to show up.

19. Be mindful of any dress codes and protocols that you need to follow for your visits. Remember that an opportunity to visit your son should be focused on the visit itself. Don't get caught up. Just follow the rules.

20. Keep the conversation during visits light and friendly and sociable. Share what's happening with the family, but be mindful to keep it positive when at all possible. Don't hide things from your son, but also don't spend your visits venting or complaining about situations that your son is powerless to help fix while he's locked up.

21. Be mindful of who is on your son's visiting list. For example, if you know your son had a drug problem going in and one of his drug-selling friends is on his visiting list, it's okay for you to discuss your concerns with your son and try to come to an agreement about who should visit and who shouldn't.

22. Once there's an end to the court proceedings and your son has been sentenced, in most cases that should be the end of any financial payments to any attorneys. It's really over at that point. Let it be over. Your son is going to get people to tell him that there's hope if he gets a lawyer and does this and that. Just let it be. Don't spend a dime.

23. It's very important to have a family presence at court. Whether you realize it or not, one of the things a judge will ask is whether or not there is family there. The dynamics of a family are really important. I always made sure that my sister, my mother, and I were there. It may not change the

sentence, but if the judge sees that there is family support he or she may be more likely to involve the inmate in programs during his sentence.

24. Be honest when given the chance. Advocate for the programs and resources that you think will benefit your son during his sentence.

25. Know that there are opportunities for your son when he's in prison or jail. Don't let your son do nothing. He has to sign up for programs. Sometimes the programs won't start right away, but there's always something for him to do behind bars to better himself. Don't listen to him if he tells you there's nothing for him to do. He has to work with his counselor and figure out what fits for him. If he doesn't have his GED, then that's the place he should start.

26. If there's any hope for your son to come home and be a productive citizen, then you need to take this journey of incarceration with him.

27. For the mothers who never take a phone call, I encourage you to rethink things. I used to say, "You can go to jail if you want to, but I won't be there." Some people can hold onto that, but he was my son. I encourage you to think about what you want life to be like when he comes home.

28. I would say to any mother that unless you decide that you will never be a part of his life again, then I would suggest that you communicate and keep the family ties going so that you can get a better son coming out than who he was when he went in.

29. Focus on the environment at home when your son is away.

What can you do to ensure that when your son does come home, he's not returning to the same place he left out of? Reflect on who you allow in your space. Is everything in that space good for him? If you know he had a drug problem when he went to jail and you know there are still drugs in your circle, what needs to happen then?

30. When coming home, our young men need to be brought into a safe, responsible, drug-free, violence-free environment. Those are really the four things. He might be 30 years old, but he still needs a home until he can get out there on his own. So you need to help him come home and then transition.

31. Ask yourself if you are really welcoming him or if you are just letting him come home because he's your child and you feel you have to. Ask yourself if you're really preparing yourself to set him up for success.

32. Put your hurt away and talk to your son. Be honest and let him know how this has affected you and the family, and then move onto conversations about bigger and better things. Trust me, your son wants to know how you are feeling.

33. Above all else, LOVE, LOVE, LOVE your son. Encourage him and never give up hope. The greatest gift you can give your son is the gift of unconditional love.

# FOR YOUNG MEN

1. Know that once you've crossed the line of incarceration, it's really hard to come back from that — not impossible, but hard. So think before you make a split second decision that can change your whole life.

2. Your parents most likely have a plan for your life and it's a good idea to pay attention to that plan. Usually, when parents talk about their hopes for their children they look something like going to school, getting a good education, going to college, and then building a solid career. Rarely does the plan involve dropping out of school, using and selling drugs, and going to jail.

3. Listen to and take advice from others, but not from everybody because not everyone has your best interests at heart. If someone is offering you something that you know isn't right, then that's not a person you want to listen to.

4. Choose your friends wisely. Know who their friends are, know what their households are like, and know their parents. If you see anything early on that makes you uncomfortable, chances are that this probably isn't a friendship worth pursuing. When you walk into a house and hear a friend say "Ma, I'm home" and "Yes, ma'am" then you know that's a house with some structure. If you walk into a home and your friend automatically takes out the trash, then that's a house with some discipline.

5. Be very mindful of what people are introducing you to. It's easier to stay out of something than it is to get out of something. If you see anything that could lead you into trouble, walk away. You don't owe anybody an explanation. Just walk away. Be your own person. If you know something is not right, don't do it.

## LESSONS

6. If you have a friend who introduces you to drugs, that person is not your friend and you need to move on.

7. Communicate with a trusting adult if you find yourself being introduced to the wrong kinds of things.

8. Don't try to fit into something you're not comfortable with just to be with the popular crowd. It's okay to be different. It's okay to be an individual and stand out on your own.

9. As long as you are still breathing, it's not too late to ask for help. No matter what you've done or how deep in you may be with alcohol or drugs or a way of life that you know is not serving you, it's never too late to seek help and get your life back on track. It may not be easy, but it's always, always possible.

10. If you know your mom or another family member is visiting on your visiting day, be ready for the visit.

11. Make sure when having a visit that you make yourself look healthy and clean so as not to worry your visitor.

12. Make sure when visiting that you keep an upbeat tone as much as possible. Often things go on in the jail that might not involve you that would leave your family worrying if you shared. Things do happen, but if it doesn't directly involve you and you don't need to share, then don't share.

13. During visits, your mom doesn't need to hear about all the things you think you need. She's not coming to get your grocery list or shopping list for the mall.

14. During visits, your mom needs to know some of the pleasant things, the learning things, the steps forwards you've made

since her last visit. If you don't feel like you have anything to share during one visit, then make it your goal to work hard so that when the next visit comes around, you do have something positive to say. Sometimes, looking at goals too far out in the future can get overwhelming or discouraging.

15. As you end the visit, remember to hug your family and show your appreciation for all that they're doing to support you. Say thank you. Tell them you love them. Let them know that you are grateful for every single sacrifice they're making because of the time you're serving.

16. Be very careful about who is giving you advice when you're incarcerated. There are some really smart people in there, but they will have young people believing that if their mothers get an attorney who can try to get them out on a technicality, then that will automatically happen. Instead of using the time trying to find some technicality on which to get released, you can spend your time inside bettering yourself for the day when you will come home. If you already have your time, that's really it. Accept your sentence.

17. Make sure that you keep all of your legal documents in a safe and secure place. Also, share those documents with your mother or whoever is going to be making the calls or doing any research for you.

18. Often, your mother and other loved ones don't receive information on court dates, locations, etc., particularly if there's no attorney or a public defender involved. So as soon as you're notified of a court date, let family members and other concerned persons know in a timely manner.

## LESSONS

19. Please, please, please do not convince your mother to throw away good money when you know it's not going to make a difference. I remember giving an attorney $1,500 to write a motion that was denied, and then Terrence turned around and wrote a motion himself that got him back in court.

20. Don't compare your situation to that of the inmate next to you and don't use someone else's situation to give your mother false hope or cause her to spend money she may not have chasing a dream.

21. Allow yourself to experience the power of giving back. You might not even know what you're capable of doing because you're not being challenged. So challenge yourself to get involved in programs and use your time to better yourself in any way you can.

22. Find a good crew when you are locked up.

23. Be very mindful of things that are going on around you. If you are in the crowd and something goes down, you are part of it.

24. Believe in what is possible for your life.

# FOR SERVICE PROVIDERS

1. Don't look at the mother of an incarcerated young man as if she's failed. Instead, look for areas in which she may not be strong and then help her to address those areas.

2. Be able to provide mothers with resources that have proven track records of helping families heal and incarcerated young people become successful. For parents, one of the worst things that happens is when they reach out for help and they don't get it. Have a list of resources ready to provide the mothers with upon request.

3. If you don't know the answer to something an inmate's family member asks you, find it. Please never tell a parent that there's nothing you can do. I reached out for preventive stuff and was told time and again that there's "nothing we can do until he actually does something," which in a way actually gave him a license to do whatever he was going to do.

4. With a listening ear, listen to every word a mother says – whether a young person is stealing, coming in late, or sleeping all day. Take in as much information as you possibly can to make sure that you can best service the young man and his mother.

5. After listening, size up the type of treatment the young person may need, whether a 30, 60, or 90-day inpatient or outpatient program. Create a roadmap for the mother so she has some idea of what she can expect.

6. Let the mothers know about the support that's out there for them – let them know that they need to be more educated themselves about the depths of the addiction so that they

can better service their child. Help parents understand that addiction is a family disease — know that this might be a paradigm shift for the family, so help guide them through it.

7. Learn to listen to mothers without judgment. Some of the mothers you come into contact with might not look like what you think mothers should look like, but the most important thing you can do is listen without condemnation and seek first to understand where they're coming from, what their pain points are, and how and why they might be reaching out for help.

8. Once you do open up a good dialogue with mothers, reassure them that they're not alone in what they are going through with their sons. Let them know that coming for help was the best thing they could have done for both themselves and their sons. Make sure they know that you appreciate all they have done to love and guide their sons and that the resources you're recommending are additional supports, not replacements or punishments. They don't come to you to get beat up; they come to you because they want and need help.

9. When you suggest resources, make sure that you've checked on them and that the services you're recommending are still available and accessible. It's very frustrating to go home excited to make that phone call, only to find out that the service is either no longer available or that your son doesn't qualify. Make sure that resources are current and applicable to the needs of the family you're working with. The resources need to be tailored to whatever the situation is — the last thing a mother needs is a run-around when she's already running in circles. She doesn't need the people who she's relying on to provide her with information to send her on another wild goose chase.

10. If possible, help the family find any resources necessary to facilitate visitation. If a mother is not showing up, try to find out what barriers exist. Maybe it's transportation or childcare or finances or work schedules, but if a family isn't visiting, try to find out why so that you can help to provide the necessary resources.

11. If you are having one-on-one time with an inmate, try to find out what his direction is going to be so that you can connect him with resources that are going to help move him in that direction. During family visits, inmates want to have positive news to share with their family members about their progress — help give them opportunities to do things that they will be proud to share.

12. Get to know who the inmates are so that you can treat them as whole people. Some of them are there because they just got caught up, so given the right tools and information, they can overcome the challenges of their incarcerations.

13. Emphasize to the inmates who do not have high school diplomas that they should use their time to earn their GEDs or diplomas. Make it a point to encourage them to leave with something more than they came in with in terms of their education.

14. If you're a part of the process of court, give insight to the mother about what's going to happen and what the possibilities are, and warn her that her son might not come back out of that courtroom.

15. Prepare the mother for the next phase after her child has been taken into custody — where he'll be housed, when he'll

arrive there, what the holding process is like. Inform her about any anticipated gaps in communication, delays in getting to where he'll be housed, etc.

16. Be available during the first part of the incarceration for any questions the mother may have, such as what can her child have, are visiting days even or odd, what time are visiting hours? Make the transition as smooth as possible for the families. Try to listen and be a voice. Even if the information is readily available, understand that some families are going to want a human connection to the process. Be available to provide that when possible.

17. Be mindful that not everyone has internet access or the ability to look up information for themselves online and that they might find it easier or more comfortable to pick up the phone and call.

18. If you can't help a young man with whatever situation he comes to you with, make sure that he doesn't leave the meeting unsure as to who can help him. Connect him with the appropriate person and then follow up to make sure that he actually got connected with the person you referred him to.

19. Remember that not all inmates are hardened criminals and most of them are savable – with your help.

20. Be a giver of hope, a believer in dreams, a bright light in a sometimes dark world.

Figure 1: Bettye, Terrence, Brandee, Gran & Marcus

Figure 2: Brandee, Shantell & Terrence

Figure 3: Terrence, Brandee & Brandee's Parents, Betty & Marcus

Figure 4: Brandee & Terrence, Wedding Day May 1, 2001

Figure 5: Terrence, David Miller & Youth Challenge Participant

Figure 6: Terrence, Brandee & Shantell

Figure 7: Terrence & Brandee

Figure 8: Terrence & Granddaughter Amari

Figure 9: Granny Willa Mae Cain

Figure 10: Dink, Tonie, Terry, Karen, Salliey, Shauna & Gran

Figure 11: Guys from the Youth Challenge Program, Hagerstown, MD

Figure 12: Shantell, Amari, Brandee, Alayah & Terrence

# BOOK TWO
## THE VILLAGE

STICKS IN A BUNDLE ARE UNBREAKABLE.
— KENYAN PROVERB

# INTRODUCTION
## TO THE SECOND BOOK

What follows are excerpts from the many interviews that my editor conducted with family members and experts in the field of incarceration and/or addiction. They represent just a small glimpse into the village. None of us are an island, and even though this journey was about me and my son, these interviews provide additional insight into the love and strength that surrounded us and continues to surround us.

**EDITOR'S NOTE:** *The original intent was to blend all the voices you'll see in the pages that follow into the main narrative of the First Book. But like so many things in life, sometimes your original destination is not where you were intended to head. For reasons both intentional and organic, we decided that these interviews, these voices, stood most powerfully as raw and true to their original form as possible. The phone and video interviews were unstructured in nature, which means I didn't go into any of the conversations with a particular agenda or set of structured questions. Thus, I made the decision to not include the interviewer's questions as part of the interviews you'll read so that the focus remains on the perspectives and opinions and truths of those with whom I spoke and not on the questions I asked. My role was just that of a guest, welcomed into a home* *and a family and a space not my own for brief interludes. We've also included a couple of letters that were written to Terrence during his incarceration. The beauty and power of these letters needs no explanation.*

# PART I
# THE FAMILY VILLAGE

YOU DON'T CHOOSE YOUR FAMILY. THEY ARE GOD'S GIFT TO YOU, AS YOU ARE TO THEM.
— DESMOND TUTU

# **1**
# **BRANDEE**
## TERRENCE'S WIFE

Terrence and I met in October of 1998 at the BWI Airport. I was in college and working an internship with the airport security department and he was working at the airport as well. He happened to come through the security terminal one day when I was working and we started talking and exchanged phone numbers.

We connected instantly and became good friends quickly. I was 20 at the time and he was 24. Terrence was very attentive and we talked a lot on the phone. Only one week after we met, my brother-in-law was in a major car accident where the driver was killed. I had to fly to California right away to be with my brother-in-law, and Terrence kept calling my mother to check up on me. I think the most impressive part was that he showed so much love, care, and compassion for me and my family, even though we had just met. From there we dated and saw each other frequently. I remember he used to just look at me when we were driving. We would go out with my girlfriends and they were just like, "Wow, he's so in awe with you."

Terrence introduced me to his daughter right away, who was 10 at the time, and she immediately became like my stepdaughter. Shortly after we started dating he came to my college graduation. He was there with my grandparents and entire family and immediately hit it off with everyone. My family fell in love with him and my mother recognized him as her son almost right away. They sensed his caring and loving nature.

Terrence always made me a priority. It was never "Let me see what the guys are doing first," but instead "Let me see what Brandee is doing first, then see what everyone else is doing." It was opposite of what I was used to seeing with guys, so it stood out to me.

I remember that when we first met he told me right away that he had a looming legal issue that he was going to have to deal with. By the time his court date came up, we had been dating six months. He got his first sentence and I was completely devastated, knowing he was going to be gone for at least three years. We weren't even a year into the relationship. I had just graduated college and was living at my parents, saving to buy us a house.

I was determined to stick it out because I was convinced that what had landed him in jail had happened years ago. I believed he was a changed person from the one who had been selling drugs and who had done whatever else went along with that sentence. I wasn't going to hold his past against him because I saw no signs of drug use with him while we were dating. Nonetheless, he went away for three years.

During his sentence, we were in nonstop contact. My life revolved around waiting by the phone for him to call, feeling anxiety if I missed a call. I felt the stress of making sure I received every call. We would talk on the phone as long as we possibly could. We would even listen to each other fall asleep because we never wanted to hang up. We would take advantage of every second we had to talk and would also write letters and send pictures. I didn't date anybody else during those 3 years. I didn't go on any dates or even exchange numbers. I was 100 percent committed to Terrence and our love. My parents went on visits to see him, and I would visit every time I could, bringing his daughter with me and staying the entire visiting time. Even when he got transferred, I would drive an hour away to visit him. It was a cycle of the anticipation of seeing him and the sadness of leaving. It felt like torture going through those metal detectors and hearing the bars slam closed. I couldn't stand seeing him locked up and being treated the way he was. In my eyes, he just didn't belong there.

We got engaged when he was away. He gave me his mother's ring. I remember being so excited and in love. I didn't even care where we were at the time. During the first three years Terrence was gone, I was like a mother to Shantell even though he wasn't there. I called Shantell's mother and would make arrangements for her to stay with my family and spend some holidays with us. Terrence wasn't around and I wasn't even married to him at the time, so that shows the kind of connection Shantell and I had. I loved her as if she was my own and was so grateful that her mother trusted me enough to allow us time to bond.

As time went on, I started planning for the wedding and our future. My mother and I would go together to look at houses and wedding venues. With all that was happening in my life, my family still continued to support and love Terrence while he was away. They wanted to support him because they saw all of his great qualities and they were not going to let his past mistakes affect their love for him. I remember my parents saying, "We won't let this change everything. We're gonna look at everything you are now and love you as a son." My parents accepted all of Terrence's phone calls and were looking forward to the wedding.

When he came home, the transition was a happy one. My parents allowed Terrence to move into his own room in their house. They were old fashioned, so we weren't allowed to share a room. He was on the lower level of the house, separate from everybody else. My mother and father showed great love in allowing him to stay in their home. As I just mentioned, they were very old-fashioned, so letting him stay in their home was a big deal.

He was on house arrest, but was able to get a job and take the bus to work every day. When he got off of house arrest, we started going together to look for a house. I used all of my savings to put a down payment on our first home and we moved in shortly thereafter. Then we got married and everything was still good, until it wasn't. I started seeing the signs, as he was coming in later or taking too long to come in. He would tell me he would be home in 20 minutes, and then would show up an hour or more after. Money started going missing out of the account.

His mother started giving me some pointers on what to look for with Terrence's drug use, and I would get irritated with her. I felt like she was trying to disrupt things, stir up trouble, and cause conflict between us. She was telling me one thing, but Terrence was in my home, in my bed, telling me the exact opposite.

Terrence appeared to function normally at first, and so it was hard to pick up the signs. Growing up, I didn't know anything about using or selling drugs, so the whole lifestyle was foreign to me. My brother-in-law, who grew up in the roughest part of the inner city, was more familiar with certain things and would point out Terrence doing things like nodding off at the table. My brother in law saw the signs, but I would blow him off like he didn't know what he was talking about.

Let me back up a bit, because there's a very important detail that I need to make sure I don't skip here. Three weeks before we got married, I caught Terrance using drugs. I remember thinking, "Oh my God, are you kidding me?" It was visible, staring me in the face. This wasn't just his mother giving me hints, or my brother-in-law educating me on the signs of drug use, this was me seeing it with my own eyes. I was so nervous and didn't know what in the world I was going to do. At that point, he said he was going to get help, and I felt like I had no choice but to believe him. I was invested in the relationship and our wedding was rapidly approaching. I had waited three years for this guy to come home, had had all this faith in him, had watched my family have faith in him, and had been saving and preparing for a whole life with this person. So I thought that I was just going to believe him one more time. I actually went with him to the drug rehab center and was willing to do anything I could to help him get the help that he said he wanted. I didn't share any of this with anyone at the time, and my confidence in both Terrence and myself was waning at this point.

So we went ahead with the wedding and our honeymoon and everything appeared to be fine. I continually asked him on the honeymoon if he was okay, if he was having any cravings, if he wanted to go home. He would of course say that no, everything was fine.

Not even a month later, the police officer was banging on our front door late one night. I was horrified. What a truly frightening experience this was for a newlywed. I was so scared. I remember calling his mother and my mother, telling them that the cops were going to probably call them next. I told them what to say to the cops, what lies to tell when questioned. Terrence was home, and he told me not to answer the door. I knew that he wasn't going to walk out of our home a free man. There was nothing we could do, nowhere he could hide.

I had a hard time coming to terms with how I had ended up in that moment. Terrence and I had had such a strong initial connection and I really did get swept up in his love. And I was young and excited about spending my future with him. I also think my not being educated about the lifestyle played a part — I was naïve a lot of the time, blind to what was right in front of me. At the same time, I think there was a lot I *didn't* want to see because all I was focused on was my dream of the house and the white picket fence, that whole fairy tale I thought I'd have with Terrence.

I finally did go answer the door and told the police Terrence wasn't home. He hid in the attic while I had this conversation at the door. I was shaking in my knees. I closed the door and the cops walked back to their cars, but I could see that they were going to wait in their cars. Then his mother calls us and says, "Listen, I just talked to the cops. Just open the door and let him go with them." The cops came back to the door and all that Terrence requested is that they not handcuff him in front of his wife. They granted him his request and led him off.

From here, the timeline gets a bit fuzzy to me. I think he got released on bail this time and I don't remember him being gone very long. I just remember him leaving and then at some point coming back home. We carried on as if nothing was wrong, even though I started to become like a detective with my own husband. I continued to see those same signs of drug use as before, and this caused me to start checking the phones and bank accounts. I had such anxiety. I remember sitting in my bed late one night, checking my debit card balance and thinking that something didn't make sense about the balance on my card. I remember asking Terrence about it and his reply didn't make sense. I may have been blind to this stuff before, but now Detective Brandee was in full force. I called the bank's 24-hour line and had the bank representative give me all the dates, times, and locations of the ATMs where my card had been used. She started naming off these locations in Baltimore city, places where I would have never gone. Some of the times of the transactions were from the middle of the night. I think that's when I realized how badly Terrence had been lying to me and when my anger kicked in.

That's when I started going through the trash cans, looking for evidence that he was using drugs. Now I knew what some of the signs looked like, I had a visual, and I wasn't as naïve. He kept denying everything, no matter how much proof I had to the contrary. Then I started to become really anal about checking the phone. I used to tell him,"Oh you're on your way home? I know it takes 20 minutes to get home from where you are." I started clocking everything, keeping track with my watch. If he took two minutes longer than I thought he should to get home, I was suspicious. I didn't know what to do with my findings, but I did feel that I had more control in an otherwise uncontrollable situation. I was coming from a place of not wanting to be fooled.

This behavior went on for a couple of months. We were into the summer by this time and he was still denying his drug use and saying he was going to get help. We would go to his mother's house together, and I noticed that he was always making some sort of excuse as to why he had to run back into the house if we were all headed out somewhere. Of course I was suspicious, but I would play along with his stories. That is, until one day I followed him back inside his mother's house, tiptoed down the basement steps and caught him hiding in between the pantry and the walls. And I remember saying, "Oh my God! I can't do this anymore. I keep believing you, but every time I turn around I find something new."

I was devastated and just started bawling and fell to the floor. I asked myself, "What have I gotten myself into? Here I keep trying to save this person, but I don't know what to do to turn him around." I had all this faith in him that he was a different person and now he was struggling with an issue that he probably had been battling with since long before we met and it took it staring at me in the face like this for it to really hit me. I felt so defeated when I realized that no matter how hard I tried, I wouldn't be able to save Terrence.

Terrence did start talking more about wanting to get help, but he was so back and forth and then would change his mind about treatment when we actually got to a rehab center. I felt like I was monitoring every single thing he did, all the time. It drove me nuts. It was consuming my whole life and had started to wear me down. I believed that if I couldn't trust or have faith in Terrence, then our marriage was never going to work.

So we started marriage counseling and I remember the therapist telling us that even though we had come to her for marriage counseling, the primary issue we were facing was a drug issue. She told me that Terrence had had a drug problem for a long time and that even though it affected me, it wasn't about me. She told me that I couldn't fix it myself. As we were going to the counseling sessions, Terrence learned more about his addiction and that it had nothing to do with me. He felt like the light was shining on him. The therapist said that she would just continue sessions with Terrence. He did end up going back to therapy, but his next session was the last one.

The following week he didn't come home one night. Of course I was an anxious mess, waking up in the middle of the night because I couldn't sleep until I know he's in the house. All that night I was like, "Here it is 2 a.m., 3 a.m., then 4 a.m." I called his cellphone. I called his mother. At some point, I drifted back to sleep until my alarm clock woke me up. I had to go to work, so I gave myself a little pep talk about how I had to get myself up and go to work, how I had to go through my normal day and take care of me, how worrying about Terrence wasn't going to fix anything. I had to tell myself that he was going to do what he was going to do and that it wasn't my fault.

On my way to work I got the phone call from some girl I didn't know, who I came to find out was the girlfriend of one of the guys Terrence was with that night. I knew before she even spoke that he had been arrested. I had that feeling in the pit of my stomach. I remember pulling over on the side of the road. I couldn't drive, my eyes were so filled with tears. We had only been married for six months at that point and I felt like a failure. I blamed myself for all the signs I didn't see, all the signs I did see and chose to ignore, and all the things I thought I should have done differently. I immediately called his mother, and she was sick to her stomach too.

Terrence had robbed a store that night. He had held up a store to get money for drugs. I was both devastated and annoyed. All I could think was, "We're not even six months in and you rob a store?! I worked my tail off for three years to save to buy a house and life ain't good enough for you? I was doing all this for us — planning our wedding, planning our life — and you turn around in six months and think that drug life is more important to you than all of this that I've worked for? And my parents believed in you, and you told us you changed? You know it's all a lie — you've been lying the whole time. We went to counseling, the treatment centers, and you turn around and commit armed robbery?! I put my life on hold for three years for you. That's not gonna happen again. I'm not doing what I did for you the first time — all those phone calls that I was so excited about, running to catch every call. This time it's going to be different."

I told him not to call me at all. I told him that I wasn't driving an hour or dealing with the stress of metal detectors and all that came along with the process in order to see him. I deserved more and had worked too hard.

After that day, I couldn't even go back to our house for an entire month. I stayed on a friend's sofa. Here I was with a mortgage, a college degree, a job, and I couldn't even go home. Our house just sat empty. One month turned into six and I still couldn't return home because our home was full of too many memories and dreams of what we had and could have had. I was so beat down and couldn't handle the thought of going home alone. My sister wanted me to stay with her, but I didn't even want to be around family. I mean, I'm her baby sister and was going through a crisis, but I had too much pride to stay with her. I was used to being the tough one, always having everything under control, always keeping everything together, always being on the straight and narrow. I didn't want anyone in my family asking if I was okay. I just couldn't handle it.

When Terrence left this second time, I was immediately protective of Shantell. I told her mother that I wasn't bringing her down to see him because I didn't want her to be exposed to that place again. I felt it was unfair to put her through the whole ordeal. I also made it very clear to Terrence that I didn't want to take his calls. Eventually, I did take a few calls here and there, but they weren't pleasant. It wasn't like, "I love you," but was more like, "What do you want?" It was night and day from the first time he was away. I was filled with nothing but anger and resentfulness and hurt by this time. I felt abandoned and I blamed him for crushing our dreams.

I stayed in counseling for many years and just didn't know how to get myself through this. I couldn't seem to pick up the pieces of my life. I started to rebel out of anger and began dating and saying mean things to Terrence. After spending many counseling sessions discussing how my moving on with my life would affect Terrence and his recovery while being away, I eventually worked up to the point where I wanted a divorce. I felt like I had spent so much time worrying about Terrence instead of focusing on myself. I questioned how Terrence could survive a divorce behind bars and who he'd have to talk to and if he was going to be okay, which is why it took me so long to follow through with the divorce.

It was about four years into Terrence's sentence that we divorced. I became determined not to put my life on hold any longer. I kept on with my career, dating, and hanging out with my girlfriends. I remember that I would keep an overnight bag in my trunk so that I was prepared if my friend Carla and I wanted to go somewhere after work. I was going to do what I wanted, when I wanted to.

Prior to Terrence's release, we had discussed that there was no hope for our relationship. I wasn't leaving the door open and was determined to live my life, knowing that our divorce was a result of his mistakes and not mine. I made it clear to him that I was dating, that he wasn't coming back home when he was released, and that he better have somewhere else to go. Throughout this whole time, I still felt in my gut that he was my soulmate, but I had resigned myself to the fact that our circumstances wouldn't permit us to be together. That realization filled me with a pain like no other.

I was putting out the impression that I was just living my life and not waiting for him. I was determined that everyone was going to know that I wasn't putting my life on hold, although really the person I was trying to convince was myself. The day before Terrence's release, there was an energy in me as I was hardly able to believe that he was coming home and that 10 years has passed. I quickly realized that my love for him had never left. I didn't know how much he had moved on and I knew he had started talking to other women. I remember I called his mother from work, asking if he had arrived home yet. I still didn't know if I wanted to be with him, but I was filled with excitement that the person I loved was coming home.

He called from his mother's house later that day and I went there straight from work. We hugged, talked, and went on a walk. He told me he was angry with me, and we went through the blame game. I told him that he had a drug problem and he told me that I shouldn't have been dating other people before we were officially divorced. So we had that back and forth of who was right and who was wrong and for the longest time we couldn't get past that. I believed that the root issue was with him and that

I felt it wasn't my obligation to put 10 years of my life on hold for this person who said he was going to change and didn't.

So we started counseling. He didn't move in with me right away. I visited him at his mother's and he dated other people. I didn't. I realized I wanted to be with him and I started to notice changes in him. He started to talk about goals, and I witnessed a change in his habits, friends, and conversations. It was a new man before me. After many counseling sessions and long talks, we knew in our hearts we were meant to be together. We had so much history. We shared so much. We were best friends. We decided to get married again, and this second time it felt like I was marrying the person I really loved. The man God sent for me. Our first wedding seemed in many ways fake in comparison to the second. The first man I married had drugs in his body, whereas this new person was drug free. Our second wedding was more pure and more honest. The first time we got married I had known things about Terrence that nobody knew, but by our second wedding he had told everyone honestly about his life-long problem. He really had a "come to Jesus" moment with all our families, even my cousins. He laid all his cards on the table to show everybody that yes, he did have this problem and it was a part of who he was, but that he had changed. He owned it and that's when all the doors opened up, when people could see him for the real person he was.. It was a tough fight to get to where we were. It took a lot of work, commitment, honesty, and communication on both sides, but we did it. We came out on top with many lessons learned through our struggles. Now we have a beautiful daughter and so many life lessons to teach her that we both learned from our journey.

The biggest lesson I've learned from all this is to not try and change somebody else. They have to want it for themselves and be willing to put in the work. You can't guilt them into it. They won't do it because you want them to and they can't do it for somebody else. You can't make them go to classes or treatment centers. When they're ready in their own time, in their own mind and they're committed and have really had enough, that is when change will come.

# 2
# ERIKA
## TERRENCE'S SISTER-IN-LAW

My sister Brandee and I are very different. She has always been a private person, not very emotional. She knows how to hold things in and she deals with situations as they come, whereas I'm extremely emotional. Before Terrence was incarcerated, there were many things that I did not know about him, even though my ex-husband had noticed signs of Terrence's drug use and brought them to my and my sister's attention. We grew up in a family where you didn't judge anyone and where everybody deserved a second chance, no matter what he had been through.

When I first met Terrence, I liked him right away and I never had any doubt that he loved my sister. When trouble came along, my family thought it was something very small at first because my sister didn't share the details of his criminal past when they first started dating. Her relationship was her business at the time.

The day Terrence was first sentenced, my sister called me hysterical. She was screaming and crying on the telephone and I couldn't understand what she was talking about at first. She finally calmed down enough to let me know that he had gotten locked up. At the time, she had suspicions that he had stepped outside of their marriage because he didn't come home one night. She had even gone so far as to pack all of his stuff up. She told me she was planning to put him out until somebody called her and told her that he had been arrested. I think that's when everything started to fall apart.

I think what hurt me the most is that I had believed in their relationship and had believed that Terrence loved my sister. As cliché as it may sound, when they got married I asked him to promise me that he would not hurt my sister. Six months later he was arrested. After that, I was angry and I carried that anger for years up until the year they were reunited. I felt like my sister had put her life on hold for almost seven years. It was hard for me to watch because I felt that he should have loved her enough not to have married her in the first place. I felt that he did not put her first. That was hard for me as her sister to watch because Brandee is very educated and independent. Even though I was older, I looked up to her, so to watch her be broken was the hardest thing for me.

My sister and I grew up very well we didn't have to want for anything. Brandee went to college, got a degree, bought her own house, and bought her own car. There was no reason any man wouldn't have wanted her. I think that it's important to recognize that not all women in a situation like Brandee's have nothing going for them. There are women who are doing very well and still find themselves in situations like my sister's.

When some people hear the word "incarcerated," they shy away. I get it, because I have never actually told anyone myself that my sister's husband has been incarcerated. I don't even know if

Brandee knows this. I think part of it for me is embarrassment for her and our family. I've never shared about Terrence's incarceration because I didn't want him to be in situations where he would feel uncomfortable knowing that everybody in the room knew he had been in jail.

I remember telling Brandee that she deserved to have a life, which was out of the question to her at first because she was still married. In the beginning she would tell me how she said vows "for better or for worse," but in my mind Terrence had already broken his vows and had made his choice clear. On the other hand, I understood where she was coming from because our family instilled in us that when it came to relationships, you keep your family together. I was also angry at his mother, even though Ms. Bettye and I get along well now, because she knew about his addiction and allowed my sister to continue dating Terrence. I held onto that for a long time and I don't think I released that until the year before they got married.

I was not jumping up and down about them reuniting because I was letting my anger fester. It just really hurt me to know what she was going through, but I was also inspired by her because she was so amazingly strong. I've told her how proud I am of her. When I went through my own personal trials, I looked to her and knew that in the end I would be okay, too.

Terrence came to see me in the hospital the year I was sick and I told him that I was very angry with him, even though my family was forgiving. I remember the day that he came home on house arrest, Brandee and Terrence came to my parents' house. I went out and walked right past them — just got in my car and left. I didn't speak to either Brandee or Terrence. In order for me to forgive Terrence, I had to come to understand that you can have a bad streak in life and still come out on the other side and make it.

The family support that Terrence received made all the difference in his life post-incarceration. Whether he was with Brandee or not he still had people who were there. And he really is a great brother-in-law, a great man. Anything my sister says that her sister needs, he's there. When I was ill he was there. When I needed something I knew that I could call on him. I've watched him with my niece and I think he's a great father. He's a hard worker. He puts his family first. I think that all he has experienced, even though difficult, has made him a better person.

# 3
# BETTY
## TERRENCE'S MOTHER-IN-LAW

My son-in-law Terrence is a very impressionable person. People meet him right away and feel his love and generosity. When I first met him, it felt like I had known him for a long while. Since the time he and Brandee first married, he's always called me mom. I tell Terrence that he's an excellent father and he tells me that since his father wasn't in his life much, he's always wanted to be a great dad. I make sure he knows that he is a wonderful father. Terrence is also great with his extended family, including his aunts and his nieces. He's really family oriented. For example, around the holidays he'll call and say, "Mom let's get both sides of the family together and go to a park and have a picnic." He wants to keep the family together at all times.

My first reaction when Terrence got locked up was denial, because I didn't get the impression from him that he would get himself in trouble. I always want the best for my children, and he broke my daughter's heart. She was really in bad shape, so it put me in a bad way and my denial quickly turned to anger. Even so, we stayed in touch through his entire incarceration. We wrote letters back and forth, and I encouraged him to always keep his faith and hope. I would visit him often, and whatever he asked me for — whether it be socks, soap, or anything — I'd send.

I stayed close to Terrence because he never showed me that he was a bad person. I also believed that my baby girl had a good sense about people, so if she loved Terrence then I would love Terrence. They made such a good couple from the beginning, so I thought that if my daughter was still seeing this person although he was incarcerated, then I couldn't turn my back on him. I never threw him away because I believed he was a good-hearted person who had just gotten caught up in a bad situation.

Now that he's out, he is his own person and expresses good judgment. He's dedicated to his family and is very responsible with money. He cares a lot about providing well for his family. His mother was always there for him, always in his corner as far as I could see. I told him that if he started down a good road, then whether my daughter would take him back or not would be up to her. When he came out he had made such a marvelous change and that's what got them back together.

The thing is, I'm not a real forgiving person. My mother used to tell me, "Betty Jean, you just hold things so long. You just gotta let it go." As I've gotten older, I've learned that you have to be able to forgive and let things go. You can't just let things fester. And you've got to love. I tell Terrence that I love him because of the person that he is and because he has made my daughter happy. I'm most proud of the way that Brandee and Terrence have turned out together as a couple. I'm proud of how he has turned his life around and has made a wonderful life for my daughter, my grandchildren, and now my great-grandchildren.

# 4

# DAWNITA AKA "COUSIN DINK"
## TERRENCE'S COUSIN

*Dawnita wrote the following when Terrence was serving his longest, and last, sentence.*

I, Dawnita Michelle Brown, was born on February 13, 1973, a little over five months after Terrence. Our baby books were shared, our bedroom was shared, our lives were shared, as if we were more siblings than cousins. The family photo albums of Terrence and me scream "brother and sister." Although we had other cousins around the same age as us, Terrence and I shared a special bond. He was and is my only brother.

Terrence was what you would call a "good guy." He was very spoiled and had things that his friends had to hustle for. Terrence attended private school, had a college scholarship set aside for him, was gifted a brand new car at the age of 15, had all the latest fashions, and I could go on and on. Whatever he wanted, he got. As went his social life as well. He wanted to fit in with his friends, so he got a life of hustling and addiction. Good guy turned bad — bad not in character, but in decision making.

It is hard to lose someone who is not gone physically, which is how I feel about Terrence when he started to lose his way. Although we liked the same music, TV shows, and clothes and had the same friends, we made very different choices as we grew. I excelled in school, had fun and even partied hard. However, Terrence chose to do things that I would never think of doing, including using drugs. I guess he just wanted to fit in, but it broke my heart. To watch Terrence spiral downward and turn into someone I sometimes didn't even recognize was very hard for me. Releasing the disappointment that I felt toward him has been an arduous process. All I can do now is work hard to release my anger and heal. After all, he is my brother.

I commend Terrence on the work he now does with youth. I thank God that he is a mentor and role model to many young people who are on the road to destruction. I pray that he stays strong and free from the bondage of addiction. And most of all, I anticipate the day when I will find him at home with me, his sister, again.

# 5

# JOAN
## BETTYE'S SISTER

My sister Bettye is an educated woman who loves people. If you meet her once, she's your friend for life. She's bubbly, free-spirited, and good-minded and a wonderful mother, grandmother, and great-grandmother. Bettye and I are only 16 months apart and our children are like siblings. Our parents taught us to be independent and not depend on anyone else for what we wanted. That's how we grew up and became responsible for each other, even now that we're seniors. We're the same now as we were when we were young.

Speaking of family, let me tell you a little about our mom. I could talk about my mom forever. My mother didn't work when we were little, and when we were in the house she made sure there was breakfast, lunch, and dinner on the table every single day. We did our homework and knew the rules, which made it easy for us when we got out into the world on our own. I'm not going to say our mother sheltered us, but we were kept under her wing to make sure that we did what we were supposed to do. We were responsible for our children, even when we were living with my mother. In our mother's house, if your child fell — like off of a bed or sofa — before he was walking, it was the worst thing in the world to her because that meant you weren't watching your child. We had to keep our shoes white and our flannels not flying around. We had the whitest shoe strings in the whole world. Our mother taught us many things that we still use today in our lives.

My mother passed when Terrence was in jail. I think that's another thing in Terrence's life that has made him become the man he is today, because not being here with the woman who was behind him 100 percent was so hard for him. Even when she wasn't accepting of him, our mother would make peace with Terrence. I think there's that part of Mama in us — making sure that our kids are doing right and are providers and independent.

There's trouble with association and the trouble Terrence got in was with other people, but it can't be blamed on other people. One thing I appreciate and am proud of, after the whole time he was in jail, is the product now. He's responsible and he's hard-working.

My daughter, Dink, and Terrence grew up so close and have remained so through the years. I think they have an absolutely beautiful relationship. Dink doesn't have any children, but she's so close to Terrence's granddaughter Amari and his younger daughter Alayah — she couldn't love them anymore if they were her own.

When Terrence got locked up, it affected Dink a lot because II wasn't just that he was being arrested, but for what, locked up for what? I'll never forget the night, it was 2 or 3 in the morning, when Bettye came knocking on my door. I knew something had to be really wrong, since she hadn't called first. As soon as I opened the door and saw her face, I knew it had to be bad. She said four little words that changed the course of all of our lives: "Terrance got locked up." "Locked up for what?" was my very first question. I forgot what her exact response was, but she did share that she had already been out to try to bail him out, but she didn't have enough money to do so. That's why she had come right to my house, to ask if I could help her. Of course, I got right up, put my clothes on, and went right up to the police station with her to bail him out.

It was hard not only for Bettye, Mama, or Terrence, but for all of us. I think sometimes people don't realize how their actions affect the people they love. When he came home, my hope was that he wouldn't be affiliated with anyone who he had been around when he got into trouble. When he was struggling at work one day, he called me for advice and I told him, "You got a good job right now and you are around good people and you need to stick with it." He didn't say anything before hanging up, and then called me back a couple days later to let me know that he had thought about what I said and the day after our first conversation his boss had called him and given him a raise.

I'm proud of Terrence and the fact that he's a father who understands what it means to be a father because his father wasn't really in his life. I'm proud of the initiative he takes with his daughters and granddaughter. I'm proud of him for not looking back, he's looking ahead and I know if he had anything to change in his life, it would be the elimination of the years he lost in jail, and all the good times he missed with the family that he could only get through phone calls or pictures. He's very family orientated and he really missed the family. I just enjoy seeing him be a man, a father, a good husband, great nephew, great cousin to his cousin. He's all around doing what he's supposed to do. If my mother was still living, she would be very proud because he's the Terrence now that she knew he was.

# 6

# GRAN
## BETTYE'S MOTHER AND TERRENCE'S GRANDMOTHER

*The following is the last letter that Gran ever wrote to Terrence during his last incarceration. The letter was dated August 2, 2004. She passed away on August 23, 2004.*

Dear Terrence,

Just a short note to let you know we haven't forgot you. I pray you are doing the very best you can. Everyone sends love. I haven't talked to Cousin Terry. The family is doing okay. We had someone working on our house in Tillery, N.C. No luck with the Lottery. I don't play every day, only once in awhile. We'll be going to Tillery on the 20th of this month to check the house. Jeanne, Joan, and your mother are going. So Terrence take care of yourself.

Love you, Gran

Here is some change.

# 7

# ANDRE
## TERRENCE'S COUSIN

Terrence is my little cousin, a standup guy who is very dependable. He was a good kid and we used to call him the golden child because he was my aunt's only son. I think that he was a cool kid who just got caught up trying to run with the big boys.

And my Aunt Bettye? That's my girl. I call her my cousin-aunt, because she is the only one of all my aunts who doesn't care about being all proper. Aunt Bettye is a piece of work and will make her presence known on any scene. When we were kids, we used to call her the "self-imposed favorite aunt." If you said anybody else was your favorite aunt, there was going to be some trouble. My aunt used to babysit me and even though I was not the easiest kid to babysit, my aunt didn't care about me crying and whining. It didn't pay her no mind. She would sit there and whine next to me, like "Why you whining?" She would antagonize the baby.

My grandma, Gran, was a pistol and a piece of work. I guess that's where my Aunt Bettye gets it from. Gran definitely made sure her grandkids didn't go anywhere hungry. If you went over to her house, you knew you were leaving with a meal. Gran was quick of wit and quick with that tongue. You were never going to get away with saying something slick around her. She would definitely put you in your place. My grandfather was a laidback guy when we came around as kids. When all of us wild kids would come around, Big Dad, as we called him, would retreat to the safety of his room to smoke and watch his baseball games. I think he was out-shadowed by the presence of my grandmother, who was going to be the center of attention one way or another.

Unfortunately when Terrence started to get into trouble, I was already in a bit of trouble myself. So basically all the information I got about him was either second-hand news from family members or people I knew on the street. I would try to talk to him and make sure he didn't travel the road I had traveled, but somehow he went south anyway. I used to tell him to stay as far away from trouble as humanly possible because it was much easier to get into something than it was to get out of it. And that was something I didn't want for him.

For any young men who are reading this and are kind of on the edge — not yet in trouble, but on your way — I would just like to say that you do not have to choose a life of trouble. I know in our communities it's almost like a badge of honor to say you've been locked up, but there's nothing cool about it, nothing slick.

And for the families, don't let your sons fall through the cracks because not everybody's mindset is going to be "Okay, I made a mistake and I need to get myself together and go home and do the right thing." Some people fall through the cracks and become institutionalized and it becomes a way of life until they are well into their fifties and sixties. I've seen it. I urge the kids this is not really what you want. I could go on for hours about this.

And if you're reading this being in or just having come out of incarceration, this is my message for you. While you're locked up you have to find a way to improve yourself to some degree. Use the time you have available. A lot of guys, I'm not going to lie, have a hard time trying to get a start from nothing. You're going to have to sacrifice. This isn't a guaranteed formula for everybody, but I knew for myself that I had to learn something from my experience so I wouldn't repeat my mistakes. Also, if you don't have an education, get yourself some when you're away, whether it be your GED or vocational training. Persistence, patience, and sacrifice are important. You might have to work a job you don't want to work at first, but you might have to in order to get to where you want to be. The reality is that there's no written law that says you have to go back to jail or the life that you had. I won't sugarcoat it and say that it's a cakewalk to make a better life for yourself, but it's doable. There's not a one-step formula, but the more you prepare yourself the more opportunities you'll have. I would also say to change your circle of friends, because surrounding yourself with guys doing positive stuff can give the inspiration to see that if they can do it, so can you. It changes your mindset when you're around people who are doing what you want to do.

And my advice for mothers would be don't give up on your sons because when they're locked up, having that connection to the outside is so important. Don't baby them or spoil them when they're incarcerated, but make sure they know the main goal is to get out instead of accepting a life of being institutionalized. They need to know that there is a hopeful situation waiting for them on the other side of their time.

# 8

# ADRIENNE
## TERRENCE'S COUSIN

Terrence is a very lovable and likeable young man. He's always been kind and courteous, the kind of guy you write home about, the kind of guy you'd want your daughter to marry. I remember when I first found out about Terrence's sentence. I was both sad and disappointed.

In the mental health work I've done with juveniles, I've seen that young men have such a strong desire for validation — the need to be loved, to have structure, to know that there are high expectations set for them. They need to know that someone cares enough to look out for them. For anyone who works with or loves young people, make sure you find something great in them and make sure that you express to them their greatness. It may be something as simple as you saying, "Oh my goodness, you have the prettiest signature. Look at that! What else do you do? Do you paint? Have you ever tried this or that?" Encourage them and let them know that you see the goodness in them. Build that self-esteem. One of the things I talk about all the time is that the spirit is strong and resilient, and if we develop strength and resilience in our young people then they'll be able to conquer the world.

A lot of young people struggle with feelings of rejection and abandonment, and adolescents have such an innate desire to want to fit in and know that they belong somewhere. That's part of their normal growth and development. So it becomes problematic when young people feel like they don't fit in anywhere. As adults, we don't often see young people as the individuals they are. We tend to paint them all with one brush, which just doesn't work. I like to use the example of a parent who has two children and tries to treat both of her children the same, even though one child does very well with her parenting style and the other doesn't do so well. And then people might say, "But they grew up in the same home. How could they be so different?" I think that when a parenting style works for one child and not the other, it's usually because the parent didn't look at her children as they were and failed to meet their individual needs.

When I look at my cousin Terrence, I believe he felt like he needed to belong. He belonged to his family, but he didn't have that male role model that he fit with. He lost both his dad and his stepfather when he was young. He was missing a steady father figure in his life, and I think that's why he looked to the streets. That was his connection and where he felt he belonged. It's where his needs were met, I think.

All that being said, I think a lot of his success now can be attributed to his family support, along with the wisdom that comes with age and experience. I think as he's gotten older, his values and priorities have shifted. One of the things I tell parents who feel so lost is to just hold on until the lightbulb in their children comes on. If you've given your children a strong foundation, at some point they're going to get it. Don't let them go, just hold onto them until you see the light come on. The other thing I frequently tell parents is that they need to deal with their own unresolved issues. Many times the parents haven't dealt with their own issues and because their needs have not been met, then they are often unable to meet their children's needs. For example, a parent who hasn't dealt with her own self-esteem issue and might not know how to speak up for herself might be unable to teach her children how to be their own advocates. Now you're repeating a cycle that is dysfunctional. It's like the children are leaning on the parents and if the parents are broken, then the cycle of brokenness is just going to continue.

As for a mother with an incarcerated son, I would recommend counseling and self-care so that even if she's pouring out for her child, she has enough recreation, enough positivity in her life so that her body doesn't break down from all the stress. Emotionally and physically, mothers have to be equipped to meet their own needs so that they can then be there for their children.

I also think it's important for a mother to begin to really find out who her son is when he is incarcerated. What are his gifts? What are his talents? What are his interests? That way, when he comes home, you're able to best help him based on his strengths and not just what you think that he needs. And he can start building from there — is he going to be an entrepreneur and start his own business? Go back to school? With those pieces in place, he won't come out still trying to find himself. He'll have an idea before he comes back out and will have a plan that he can begin to work.

I also think that parents have to be mindful of other adults in their children's lives who may or may not be speaking life into them. It's sad to say, but sometimes even teachers, guidance counselors, and other mentors might not have the best interests of children at heart. Be attentive to what folks are saying in your children's ears. One example from my own life is when my son, who is a lawyer now, was getting ready to go into the twelfth grade. He was at the top of his class and his guidance counselor was helping him select colleges. The counselor told him not to apply to Penn State, University of Maryland, George Washington University, or any of the other top schools because she felt it was unrealistic for him to think he could get in. He was devastated and I told him, "You apply to each and every one of them!" But if my son didn't have the mother who was able to counter that negative influence, then he may have shifted his direction. I'm happy to say that my son got into every single one of those schools to which his counselor said he was unqualified. I met with the counselor and told her the potential danger that she could've caused and reminded her that in her practice it's important that she is mindful of what she says and how she guides young people. The words we speak over the lives of our young people matter so much.

# 9
# SHANTELL
## TERRENCE'S DAUGHTER

*The following letter was written to Terrence when he was serving his longest, and last, sentence.*

Dear Daddy:

Since you've been gone, I have struggled with a lot of emotions. At times I feel lost and confused with so many questions unanswered. I usually hide my feelings with a smile on my face, but lately I don't think it has been working. I miss you more and more everyday, but I hate expressing how I feel so I keep everything all bundled up. I hate that I can't call you whenever I want to talk to you. You know a daughter needs to be able to talk to her father. So much goes on in my life and the one person I need to be there for me can't be. It hurts soooo much! You have been gone a long time and it eats me up inside everyday because I miss you more than I can explain. It's crazy because this is the first time in years that I have expressed how I felt about you to anyone.

I know I'm stubborn sometimes, but one thing I want you to know is that I am very proud of what you have accomplished while being incarcerated. You went to school and have helped younger men get their lives back on track, not because you had to but because you wanted to.

Of course, I hate to see you where you are, but you're my father. And because I am your daughter I feel I should stick with you through thick and thin. When you come home, I am almost positive things will be better for both of us because we're going to have each other. I love you and no matter what happens my love for you will never change.

Love,
Shantell

• • •

My father's incarceration was hard on me, especially because I didn't get along with my step-dad. Without my dad around, I had to learn a lot of things on my own that my dad should have taught me, like how to be loved and treated by a man. As a teenager, I was both sad and angry at the situation — sad because I missed my dad and angry because I was so affected by a situation that I didn't cause.

While my dad was locked up, I went through a lot of personal things, especially with my step-dad, that I probably should have talked with my dad about. Even though my dad wasn't physically there, I could have still asked him for guidance. I just wish I could have been more understanding of his situation, because I believe we could have had a stronger relationship during the time he was gone. We lost out on a lot of time and it felt like we had to start our relationship over when he came home. It was hard then and it's honestly something we are still working on to this day. He left me when I was a little girl and came home when I was a grown woman with my own house. For a while, I felt he still treated me as if I was a little girl. I had to learn that it was hard for him to adjust to the idea that his baby girl had grown up.

For any young women going through a similar situation to what I went through, please understand that just because your father is locked up doesn't mean that he doesn't care about you or what is going on in your life. Try to always communicate openly with your father so you all can still have a relationship.

Now that I'm a parent myself, I'm focused on being open with my daughter and letting her know that she can come and talk to me about anything that goes wrong in her life. The situation my father and I went through has taught me that communication is so important. My hope is that my father and I can continue to communicate better with each other and continue to build the relationship that we didn't really have when I was growing up. I just want things to continue to grow. Sometimes we do fight when we don't see eye to eye, but we're learning to understand that we're both adults. I work hard to be a strong, independent woman who doesn't have to depend much on other people, which I know stems from everything I've been through. I was kind of forced to grow up on my own, which has helped me become a very independent woman.

I hope that anyone reading this understands that people make mistakes, but that doesn't mean they're not loving, caring, good people. My dad is just a person who made a mistake. I'm pretty sure everyone's dad loves them at some level. I just want younger people to know that just because a mistake is being made it doesn't mean that your dad doesn't love you.

And as for my grandmother Bettye, she is definitely an awesome woman who holds everything together in our family. The whole time my dad was away, she always made sure I was okay. She did a good job of holding down the fort while he was gone. I respect her a lot and am grateful that she was able to be a strong woman for herself and her family.

# 10
# DEVONIE
## SHANTELL'S MOM

I allowed Shantell to go with her grandmother and Brandee to see Terrence when he was locked up whenever she wanted to. I accepted collect calls so that she would be able to talk to him. I made sure she had a relationship with his family so that they would always be able to share with her what was going on with her father. Fostering these relationships came naturally to me because we got along pretty well. I felt it was important because Shantell was a young girl who really didn't understand what was going on and she needed a relationship with her father even though he was incarcerated.

Shantell was young when he got locked up and I don't remember explaining much to her at the time. Before he went away, they had a pretty good relationship. She would go see him on weekends whenever he asked to see her. When he was locked up, I think she was a little confused because she was so young. Her grandmother talked to her about it, but I really didn't. I let her grandmother deal with it and I just tried to be there to support her if she needed me to be, which she did.

I didn't realize at the time how hard this all was on her because she didn't speak of it a lot. When he first got locked up she would cry about it, but other than that she kept a lot of it balled up deep inside of her. The one regret I have is that I didn't encourage her to express herself more. I talked with her, but I didn't talk to her in depth like I should have. I think conversations between parents and children about how they all feel in a situation like this one are really important.

I feel like Shantell's life would be different now if her father hadn't spent those ten years behind bars. It affected her relationships and her ability to trust as she grew up.

What helped me through was that Terrence and I had put our feelings aside and had become friends before he got locked up, so Shantell knew we had no animosity toward each other. It was hard to put my feelings aside, but I did because I didn't want Shantell to see me angry.

Of course jail is not a nice place for a child to visit, but children don't even look at that because they're just happy to see their parents. As long as Shantell wanted to visit her father, I let her go. I knew he was coming out eventually and she needed to have a relationship with him. In return, he made sure he called to make sure he was a part of her life. I think that helped too and I always allowed for her to talk to him even if he had to call collect.

# 11

# SHERRIE
## BETTYE'S BEST FRIEND

I sit here and just marvel at what Bettye's been able to accomplish. You never get an "Oh, woe is me" act from her. That's just not who she is. Bettye is a very loving, giving, and confident woman. She's one of those people who would do anything for you.

We first met in 1980, I believe, when I attended a work training by myself. I was 19, far from home, and staying alone in a hotel. She stirred up a conversation with me at the front desk where she was working at the time and from that first conversation she took to looking after me during my stay. We were just shy of being strangers and she told me, "Here are the keys to my car. Go on out there and have some fun." I was amazed by the trust she had in me after hardly knowing me at all and we've been friends ever since.

Bettye is a strong woman. She holds herself together under pressure for her family — from Terrence's incarceration, to her own open heart surgery, to the death of her mother. She keeps moving forward because she has to. She perseveres by her positive attitude. She's had incredible health challenges and has the scars on her body to prove it, but she ain't trying to hide them. She walks around proud with her cleavage showing, scar across her chest and all. Bettye is bound to be the life of the party and the most beautiful person walking into any room.

Terrence is a sweetheart. I've known him since he was young and I think he is a very strong-willed individual. Right now he is working hard, he is driven, and he is trying to create a life for him and his family, but I saw his incarceration take a toll on Bettye. I think it was hard for her. It was a long trip to visit him from Baltimore. I would take her up there sometimes because back then she didn't have the most reliable transportation, but she had to make sure she saw her son on a regular basis. She never hesitated to make sure he was well taken care of and had what he needed.

# 12
# BISHOP JOSEPHINE AKA "JOJO"
## FAMILY BISHOP

I've known Bettye for approximately 12 years. We met through a friend of mine who brought Bettye to our church. From the time she first walked in, I could see that Bettye was a lively and bubbly person. I would have never known she was experiencing some of the things she was going through both physically and emotionally. She does very well, not by hiding her challenges, but also not by always bringing them to the forefront. Bettye is not the type of person who always needs to let everyone know when she's going through something.

As a matter of fact, once Bettye came to the church, she was almost never absent on Sunday mornings. I do remember one Sunday when she called me very early and said to me, "Pastor I'm in the hospital." That's when I found out that she had some health problems, including having had two triple bypasses within a month of each other. I think it was a little bit before then that I found out about Terrence and her journey with him through prison.

My children happen to have known Bettye and Terrence from before she and I met, and they told me that when Terrance started to go the wrong way Bettye did everything she could to pull him back to where he needed to be. After I visited Bettye in the hospital, I asked her if she was in anyway upset about the trouble her son has been in, and she told me that no, she had learned how to endure. Even when she would tell me that she felt like giving up sometimes, she never did. Bettye used to drive up on the weekends to see Terrence, even though she doesn't even like to drive around the corner. So it was a big deal for her to drive 100 miles to go encourage Terrence and do things to make sure that when he got out of the correctional facility he would have a chance.

Bettye is just a stormtrooper. Many times I've said to her, "I don't know if I could've done the things that you've done." She has a very positive outlook on life. No matter what.

This book is personal to me, because I have a grandson who is incarcerated and Bettye has given me so many pointers. She has taught me to encourage him no matter what, even though I get angry sometimes because I helped raise him the right way and he still went in the wrong direction. I remember one time I told Bettye that because Terrence had been raised right and had been given the best of everything, I couldn't understand how he had fallen into such trouble. She replied, "I don't understand either, but it's not for me to understand." Bettye has reminded me that even if I'm angry with my grandson, I still need to drop him a note to let him know that I'm behind him. I've heard her give other women advice too, like "Go see your son even though he's been transferred further away because he did something stupid in prison. Just put aside your anger and go see him anyway."

Through the years I've seen Bettye get angry with Terrence, read him the riot act, and then be right there for him the very next day. Bettye never allows her journey with Terrence to be interrupted by her health or anything else for that matter.

Bettye has a wealth of knowledge when it comes to advising mothers on what to do when their sons go the wrong way. The fact that she readily shares her wisdom with so many gives me hope, especially for those who might want to throw a pity party for themselves. Bettye doesn't want to have a pity party with you. She wants to encourage you because she knows how important it is.

My advice to young men who are just coming out of incarceration and getting back into the real world would be this: *Look straight ahead, I don't care what's going on to the right or to the left or what's behind you. Look straight ahead.* Young men can learn a lot from simply paying attention to the path that Bettye and so many other amazing women and men are directing them down. They can gain so much from knowing there are people willing to support and guide them as they rediscover themselves. I know a much older man who said it took his mother dying when he was 51 to realize he had to stand on his own two feet. I pray that the men who read this understand that they don't have to have a loved one pass away to realize the importance of this kind of love in their lives.

Bettye still shows Terrence tough love, even though he is successful now. He started with a small job and then got involved with a business that hired formerly incarcerated men. It wasn't long before he landed the very good job that he has now. He remarried his wife and has a wonderful little girl. To some guys Terrence's life might seem like a fantasy, but it's real. I think everyone can learn something from listening to Bettye's and Terrence's story. In reading this book, young men will come to believe that they too can be successful if they are willing to put in the hard work needed to do so. It takes perseverance and a willingness to appreciate the people who supported them no matter what. I don't even know if Terrence knew about all the times Bettye was ill. I heard her say one time, lying in a hospital bed, "I'm going to pull out of this because I got something to live for." I hope that this book inspires young men and their mothers to never give up hope because they, too, have something to live for.

# PART II
# THE COMMUNITY VILLAGE

IT IS EASIER TO BUILD STRONG CHILDREN
THAN TO REPAIR BROKEN MEN.
— FREDERICK DOUGLASS

# 1

# DAVID MILLER
## RUNAWAY SLAVE AND FOUNDER OF THE DARE TO BE KING PROJECT

I think there's a need for service providers to better understand the impact of mass incarceration on entire families and communities. The crack cocaine epidemic of the late 1980s clearly illustrates how crack hit urban communities and changed the game in terms of increasing levels of violence, fatalities, and mandatory minimums of lengthy sentences. I don't think a lot of people, particularly service providers, fully understand the speed at which a young person can go from school to prison. It's a phenomenon. I just don't think enough educators, clergy, and other folks on the front lines know enough about mass incarceration.

Secondly, people need to better understand the connection between incarceration and trauma. Many people deal with multiple traumas at young ages, which places them in situations where violence becomes a necessary way to protect themselves and their families. The generational impact that violence, poor decision making, and incarceration have on families often can be directly related to trauma. Trauma doesn't only result from seeing a stabbing or shooting. Witnessing your dad being drug out of the house and not seeing him for 12 years is traumatic. Growing up as an African American male in Baltimore, Philadelphia, or Chicago and being raised solely by women without any strong male mentors around is traumatic.

As for mothers of incarcerated young men, I think the message is to not give up on your children. I think too often we just give up — out of sight, out of mind. And I understand mothers can get frustrated, but the reality is that the vast majority of men and women come home from prison to little or no family support. It's very difficult to get family support at the deep level that it's needed. I'm not talking support in terms of helping you get your ID or a job, but real support that these young men need upon reentry. If they can't rely on family, then the road to healing becomes extremely difficult, if not impossible.

And as for what the young men need, again, I think, family is key. For example, for four months I traveled every Sunday to upstate New York to work with boys ages 14 to 18 who were serving felony charges. We knew that these boys were engaging in criminal activity very early in the game and that many of their parents had turned a blind eye to their son's activity and/or didn't understand the magnitude of their son's behavior. We heard things from families like, "He's 11 and smoking weed and I'm not gonna hustle him because at least he's smoking weed in my house" or "At least he's selling weed and not crack cocaine or heroine."

Part of the message to parents has to be that you have to be a lot wiser from a prevention standpoint. You have to be proactive and know what your son is getting involved in, whether it be hanging with a negative peer group, smoking marijuana, or being promiscuous. If your son starts smoking weed at 11, by 16 he's probably going to be addicted. As a parent, you might be working two jobs, but you have to be in tune with some of the challenges your son might be facing. If you recognize that at 11 he's not going to school, he's being disrespectful at home, and he's involved with activities that aren't going to help him, what do you do as a parent? From a prevention standpoint, he might need to go to a mentoring program.

I'm involved in a project in Baltimore where we work with over 50 young Black and Latino males who are incarcerated. Over 50. Of these young men, 7 of them didn't have a good relationship with their fathers when they were younger and the rest didn't have any relationship with with their dads to the point of not knowing their fathers' names or even what they looked like. A tremendous void is created for these young men when they grow up without a sober, responsible, spiritually-guided father or father figure in their lives. Boys are supposed to learn from their fathers and their fathers' work ethics how to navigate their communities and the broader society, whereas girls learn from their fathers how men are supposed to treat women. No mother can fully replace a father in teaching her son how to navigate the community. When that father figure is absent, it creates issues around identity formation, an understanding of manhood, and a general anxiety around what's my place in the world. A lot of boys go through the process of being a boy to a man without ever realizing that one of their major challenges has been not having the benefit of growing up with a mother and a father and benefiting from both masculine and feminine energy. It's a problem not only in urban communities of color, but even in white communities where an increasing number of fathers are leaving their families. It is a problem in communities of all incomes, not just low income ones. There's a crisis in this country related to father absence that most people don't talk about.

I think what makes this a phenomenal story is to look at how Terrence is doing now. It provides hope. A lot of times when you look at a situation like Terrence's, it tends to look hopeless. And then it begins to be hopeless. I've been pushing Bettye for years to do this book because the issue of incarceration and the affect it has on families, next to racism, is America's Achilles' heel. We incarcerate more people than anybody else in the entire world, and the collateral damage of this phenomenon is its effect on the family.

Most folks have burned so many bridges by the time they are released from prison, so they come home and don't even have a place to stay. When you can't go to a parent's or grandparent's house, you end up in some sort of transitional housing. Terrence had the benefit of coming home to a family who forgave him for his transgressions and approached him with a clean slate. He faced not an environment of, "You wronged us, you hurt us," but rather one of "We are gonna give you a second chance. If you need family members to take you to the job interview, we're gonna do that. If you need bus fare we're gonna do that."

Bettye and Terrence's story isn't ordinary. I've had many friends who have come home from incarceration to situations where they haven't had the family support that Terrence has had. That's why I think this story is so beautiful and important. The recidivism rate among adults nationwide is about 82%, and I think this statistic has to be attributed in large part to the lack of family support many people have upon reentry.

What often comes up with the organizations that I have a relationship with that are working on black male development, whether federal, local, or philanthropic, is the importance of the parent piece, both on the re-entry and mentoring sides. I'm working to get folks to understand that you can't work with the reentry population if we're not working from a family strengthening model. When someone is coming from prison, are they going to a halfway house, are they homeless, or are they coming home to a family?

# 2

# CAMERON MILES
## DIRECTOR OF MENTORING MALE TEENS IN THE HOOD

Since 1996, I have run a group mentoring program for male teens in the hood on Saturdays. We started with five young men and today we have served over 3,500. We began with the notion that if we can teach young men to get along with and respect one another, then maybe there won't be so much carnage on our streets through gun violence and stabbings and so on.

The biggest complaint that I've received from boys over the years is some iteration of, "Mister I'm pissed off and angry and hate life because my father is not in my life." I'm not trying to replace anybody's father, but young men need to know that there are people outside of the family who care about them and want them to be well. So I started inviting speakers in to work with the boys because I knew that seeing positive role models at an early age might make a difference in the young men's lives through exposing them to people from all walks of life. In order to get along in this thing called life, you need to be able to interact with all kinds of people. So the young men are getting to meet orthodontists, anesthesiologists, and legislators, people from every avenue and every facet you can think of.

We take field trips. We've gone to Harvard, Princeton, Yale, Morehouse, Delaware State, Hampton University, Springfield College, and Columbia. Our hope is that if the young men see that there's more to life than just Baltimore and their hoods, then they'll be more likely to stay out of trouble so that they can experience the world beyond their immediate environments.

We go to local restaurants because I think it's important for young people to learn about fine dining. The best many of them can do is a chicken box or box of yakime. When we take field trips we stay in hotels, and many of our boys have never stayed in a hotel prior to these experiences. We incorporate other cultural experiences into the college trips as well. For example, when we went to Columbia University last summer, we also visited the Apollo Theater and the Schomburg Museum, took a cruise up and down the Hudson river, and went to Rucker Park where some basketball stars have played through the years. They got a charge out of that.

I want to share with people that even though our young men may seem hard at first, at the end of the day they're all looking for love and it's important they find this love in the right place. We want them to find it in a place where there are receptive adults who are authentic and are willing to connect with the boys where they are, who know their lingo and understand their communities. Young people can sense when adults are fake, don't care, or are just showing up to a job for the money. We have to make sure that we really want to be in this work and that we're good listeners. Many of our young people have a lot to say, but many adults are just not listening. Consistency is also very important. You can do more harm than good by saying that you want to work with young people, and then after a few months are like, "Man this sh** is not for me." Once young people start to connect with mentors, they are trying to believe in and respect the partnership. We only get so many opportunities before a disappointed young man decides to join a gang or get into the drug game and start using. It's very important that mentors are sincere, serious, and dedicated to the work.

Some of our young people have adults tell them not to do x, y, z and then they see their parents or guardians sitting at a table snorting some powder up their nose. Their logical response when questioned as to their own decisions is, "How can you tell me not to do something when I saw you doing it last night?" There are young people who are raising their siblings because one parent is deceased or incarcerated and the other is on drugs. Some of these young people sell dope or their bodies in order to just survive. This is why as mentors we have to be open and receptive. If you're not willing to be a good listener and show up consistently, they I don't think the calling of mentorship is for you.

For any family members of young men reading this, reaching out and finding a program that or individual who can work with your child is crucial. If there's tension between you and your son, continuing to grind that ax won't be healthy. A third party involvement can be crucial in helping to prevent young men from acting out in response to conflict with their own parents. As a third party, I'm very firm and disciplined. I'm not here to be young men's friend. Too many parents are trying to be friends with their children, but as adults we have to be the responsible ones. I'm not going to say everything they want to hear, but I do keep it real.

I think that a lot of parents don't know how to talk to their children. If you're always angry and cursing at your son, then what else does that child know? What else does he learn? At some point, your son is going to start cursing back at you and when the child goes out of the home that's how he's going to respond to others around him because that's all he's heard in the house. We have to be very careful in raising children as to what we do and say because it's going to be regurgitated and/or mirrored at some point. We're either giving them positive things to imitate or them negative things.

We have a mantra in my organization where we say – and then the young men repeat back, "I am somebody. I am a king. I have self-worth. If it is to be it is up to me." I think the more we hear positive affirmations, then the less time we have for negative interactions. They hear the positivity in our meetings and they see positive adults around them so that they can start to think early on about what they want to do with their lives. That's why it's important to have the dentist, the orthodontist, the lawyer, the judge, the legislator, the business owner, and other professionals with different backgrounds come in each month to speak.

For mothers who have acknowledged that they need help with finding support and resources, I would tell them to get to a computer – even if they have to go to a public library to do so – and Google mentoring programs in their area. They can also reach out to social service organizations. Referrals come to me from Social Services, the Department of Juvenile Services, and the school system's Office of Suspension Services.

In my work I am most proud of the amount of success we have seen through the years. We have many young men in high school and quite a few who are working or in college. That makes me very proud. I'm also proud of the fact that we don't get any major grants and most of my donations come from individuals like John and Jane Doe who send in $50 or $100 to support our programming. I pride myself on that because if I wasn't running a good program, people wouldn't want to give money. All we can do is plant seeds and hope that they will do great things, but in order to see what our young men are capable of we have to make the time and energy to work with them, talk with them, listen to them, challenge them, and invest in them.

# 3

# JEFF NORFLEET
## PROGRAM ASSISTANT AT A RESIDENTIAL TREATMENT PROGRAM

I have experience with young men who face addiction and who have been caught up in the law. You don't wake up one day and say "I want to be an addict." It's a learned behavior. My particular experience came from me just trying to find myself at an early age, trying to fit in with all of the wrong people, and being exposed to all of the wrong stuff. A lot of the time you compensate a feeling or an emotion that comes from being hurt, neglected, or abandoned. You can be in a household with a family and the family can be loving and caring, but if you're not getting the attention you think you need, then you're going to go elsewhere for it. A lot of young people today gravitate to the streets and they're going to use because that's what their friends are doing.

There's nothing except bad things that can come from any addiction, but from my experience drug use is the worst. It's not until the addiction takes a hold of you physically that it becomes scary. Using some drugs, including heroin and other opiates, becomes very physically painful. For a person who hasn't used drugs and who is on the outside looking in, it might be easy to just say, "Well, the addict just needs to stop using." But nine times out of 10, an addict wants to stop using, but withdrawal causes them to go right back to using. When an addict is going through withdrawal, he or she tends to look for something to take away the pain. You cry out and want to stop, but just don't know how. And if you've already been shunned by the people that you love, you stop wanting to go to them and tell them how you're feeling just to hear them say, "I don't want to hear that" or "You're better than that." That's just going to make you feel even worse. It's really hard.

From my own personal experience and from what I've heard from other recovered addicts, the gratification comes from knowing that you don't have to ever relive any of that pain again once you get clean. But getting and staying sober takes work. It takes work to really sustain abstinence because when things don't go your way or when things seem tough for you, it's tempting to run back to what's familiar. Once you enter a life of addiction, it consumes your whole life.

It's curious to me how addiction and recovery are often portrayed by the media. I see commercials on TV that talk about how someone used to be an addict and now they're not. But I don't see it that simply. Even though I'm sober, my addiction hasn't gone away. It's just been arrested. And it's only arrested as long as I put the work in myself and persevere through all of my endeavors. I've had to learn how to sustain a network of people that I can talk to when I'm feeling low, and it's helped keep me sober.

I think that's what recovered addicts do well — we talk to each other and disclose personal experiences and feelings, only to find out that nothing we went through or felt was that unique to begin with. We find out that there are other people just like us, which lets us know that we belong. I've worked with people who come into treatment without a GED or diploma or and who go on to earn their doctorates after recovery. I think that's the hope in all this — that it's possible to go on to do great things. That's what I've done and that's what I advocate for others.

I also believe, and I know some people in the recovery community disagree with my stance, that if a person uses after he become clean it's because he didn't do the work. I know people say "Don't ever say 'never again,'" but I do say "Never again." Do I think about using? Yes. After using drugs for almost 20 years, it's normal for a recovered addict to think about using again. Staying sober is an ongoing challenge and something that I know I'll have to deal with for the rest of my life.

There are some people who might become sober from drugs and still drink casually, some who might not go to meetings, and some who might choose an outlet like church over recovery meetings. I believe that the key to sobriety is to grasp hold of something to remind you that you're not alone. One of the main reasons addicts begin to use in the first place is that they feel so alone. When a substance can make you feel comfortable, even if it's just for a moment, then that's what you want.

I'm adamant about recovery and about education. I believe it's really important for people who have never used to understand that a life of addiction is not something that someone consciously chooses for themselves. Want me to tell you what being an addict is like? I was married and in treatment, but wasn't open at the time to learning much of anything about recovery, so I used again after coming out of prison. My ex-wife is a doctor, so she put me in treatment again after I got out. I was in treatment with football players, doctors, lawyers, and other people from every walk of life. You have athletes who get addicted to painkillers, little old ladies who have to go to the pharmacy to get their drugs, and people like me who get addicted to street drugs. No matter where you come from, getting sober is hard work. A doctor or other professional who is prominent in the community isn't going to tell you that he got a divorce because his wife got tired of him using valium all the time. There's so much more to addiction and recovery than what many people see. People often see the drug addict on the corner or the drug addict in the market who can't control his equilibrium and is off course. And people look at the addict and judge him, but it's not fair to judge because you don't know what this person had to go through to even end up where he is.

I know Terrance and he's doing great right now. He's raising his younger daughter, working, enjoying his wife, and enjoying his new life. But these are the things that happen only if you really want them and work for them. You have to endure all of the pain, and once you get past the pain of the destruction, you have to understand yourself at a deeper level. You have to believe that you can get and stay sober and that you can actually live on life's terms without having to be sedated. I've learned that I don't have to sedate myself because I feel badly today, all I have to do is talk about how I feel. But when you don't have a healthy outlet or someone to turn to, then it can be hard to know what to do on the difficult days.

I suffer from abandonment issues like most addicts I know. It's like the people we feel we should get the most love from are the people we feel rejected from. It happens when a child grows up hearing, "You're never going to be anything." If you hear that all the time, then you're going to believe you're not going to be anything, especially when things aren't going right in your life. A lot of times the rejection from family can cause such turmoil and reign havoc in a fragile individual's mind. It doesn't have to be a child, it can be a grown adult who doesn't know how to handle his feelings and emotions. Most of the time, a lot of us don't know how to deal with our feelings and emotions. To have somebody we love and care about dearly tell us they don't want us anymore can be a hard one to swallow for someone who's not equipped to move on. Moving on is not so easy for a person who doesn't know how to move on.

Sometimes you have families that don't even use the word love, so if you're not taught how to love or practice love, how are you ever going to know what love is and how are you going to begin loving yourself? Loving yourself means that you care for yourself. Addicts in the street who use every day to the extent that they begin to get abscesses and don't take care of their bodies do not love themselves.

The key is that we have to encourage each other, especially our young people. We have to help others feel worthy so that they can then begin to feel worthy about themselves. You have to let people know that they mean something and they're cared for in order for them to begin to care for themselves.

Personally, I didn't come from a dysfunctional family. We had the normal family arguments, but I made a conscious decision to do something against my mom and the rest of my family when I chose to go out and try to fit in with what everybody else was doing. I got lost in the streets. There wasn't a day that went by in prison that I didn't think about all of the wrongs that I did. I still to this day evaluate all of my actions. I evaluate how I am in a relationship opposed to watching what another person does. It's never about the other person, but always about how you respond to a person.

Addicts have to learn how to work through their feelings. Often times if they can't get through what they're feeling, then they will return to where they came from. You have to practice loving and respecting yourself and those you love, and this can be hard for an addict. Using stunts your growth. If you use at an early age and you stop when you're older, then you have not grown emotionally during the time you used. It's like starting your life all over again. You hear most addicts say when they pray, "Thank you God for letting me live two lives in one lifetime."

Most poverty stricken neighborhoods suffer from addiction the most. People are so used to just surviving and not living. As an addict, you often don't experience everyday life things because it can take all your effort just to get what you need to make yourself feel better. Using takes away from all aspects of living. Once you're caught in the grips of your addiction, using becomes your sole method of coping. It's such an ugly stigma to think once an addict, always an addict. I don't believe that. I believe addiction is contingent on the individual's desire to recover. At recovery when you're thirty days clean, you're physically sober. Now you have to work on the mental sobriety. The mental aspect is what keeps people drawn to using, in my opinion.

It's important for loved ones of addicts to realize that even though they might not be using, they may still exhibit some of those old behaviors. Behaviors are hard to let go of once you've been practicing them for a long period of time. That being said, even if an addict is displaying some of the same behaviors that he did when he was using, if he is working on his sobriety and staying clean then he needs to hear that you support him. An addict doesn't want you to ridicule him or bash him for everything that he does wrong when he is working on bettering himself. You've got to be a little more lenient, caring, and understanding, especially when it's hard for you to understand. Asking a simple question like "How do you feel?" opens the door to a lot of stuff. It's important to all of us, I don't care what we're going through, to feel that we're important enough to be asked how we feel.

# 4

# WALTER LOMAX
## EXECUTIVE DIRECTOR OF THE MARYLAND RESTORATIVE JUSTICE INITIATIVE

After having served 40 years, I believe it is essential to give family members an opportunity to discuss how their loved one's incarceration has impacted or is impacting them. This concept is relatively new to the discussion, but it's very important. I had firsthand experience with how a family is affected by incarceration. My situation was a bit different because my family knew I was innocent, but they still had to deal with the fact that I was incarcerated. There were a lot of emotional rollercoasters through the years and some folks may have never even realized how much my incarceration affected my family.

Restorative justice begins with the person acknowledging his responsibility and what it was that lead him to his incarceration. This acknowledgement is the first step to healing. The next step involves him realizing how much his actions have impacted the person he's done them to. When he begins to see things from that perspective, it can shed new light on the situation. It allows him to be open and honest about his situation as a human being and to realize his own humanity and the humanity of those he's harmed. We do understand that some wounds are really difficult to heal and that's something that we talk about as well.

Even though I may be remorseful for something that I have done, the person that I've done it to may not be as forgiving, and I say that because I lost my brother who was murdered in 1982. Then I had a grandson who was murdered in 2006, the year I was released, and I was able to deal with that differently than my other family members. My grandson's death is an emotional wound that's still relatively raw for some of them. I know forgiveness is a difficult process, however, from a personal perspective I was able to heal because I forgave that person for what he had done. I didn't forget what he had done and I felt that he needed to be punished, but I was able to forgive him for it, and then I was able to heal myself. I try to work with other family members in that respect, too. To date I haven't been completely successful, but I know it's a difficult process.

At one point, I believe our society was more forgiving than it is now. A person would commit a crime and serve his time, deal the deal, and then return back into the community where he was able to acclimate and go on with his life. Even though he may have been impacted by the criminal justice system, it wasn't something that stayed with him for the rest of his life. Then there was a culture shift that brought with it a mindset of, "Well lock them up and throw away the key 'cause people just don't change." The myth of that is that people *do* change. There are statistics that indicate some people age out of crime after a certain time period. They just age out! I'm using that data to deal with the juveniles and the information we have now includes neuroscience research. It shows that as you mature, you begin to see things differently. Yet some people still adhere to the concept that if you committed a crime, then that's something indubitably connected to your character and will never ever in your lifetime be erased. And that is just not so. I think that's something that maybe needs to be worked on a little bit more, especially here in Maryland.

When I went to prison, the Maryland system was very archaic, stuck back in the 19th century somewhere. But we've been able to bring the system into a completely new era where educational programs became a part of the process. This change has come as a result of a number of progressive movements. Maryland has what's called "parole expectancy" built into its system, which means that if an inmate can progress through the system, then he hopefully will be paroled out eventually. At one point there were not even any reentry programs built as part of the process to allow inmates to be successful in returning to society, so we've made some progress in this area as well. Without reentry programs, you've just created this revolving door. The challenge is that even with some reentry programs in place, we've still seen prison populations nearly double in the U.S. over a ten-year period.

Those with loved ones incarcerated can find value in a guide that helps teach them what to expect in dealing with the criminal justice system. Bettye shared a story with me about the preparation that she used to use when she would go to visit her son. She said she had perfected it to such a degree that she was prepared to help other people, and in fact she actually did that over time. I had a personal experience with that when my daughter was coming to visit me on a family day once. She was normally there every time on time and we had a chance to spend a few hours together with other family members, but this particular family day she was extremely late and I was almost on the verge of having one of the C.O.s make a phone call to see if something had happened to her. She eventually showed up and when she showed up she had this lady with her. I asked her what had taken her so long and she told me that they wouldn't let the lady in because she didn't have on the appropriate attire, so my daughter had left and taken the lady to a store to buy something to wear so that she could come into the institution. People need to be aware that those situations occur and that you are not alone if you experience or witness them yourself. This is why it's so important to share our stories.

The conversation right now surrounding incarceration, especially incarceration of boys and young men, may need to revisit the concept of actually rebuilding an individual once he is impacted by the criminal justice system and understanding what it was that caused him to be institutionalized in the first place. Then I think we can move forward and assess what some of their real basic needs are in order to develop programs to meet those needs rather than just warehouse individuals. For those who come to prison receptive, the prison system should begin preparing them for their release. I don't understand it, but I do have some information on why they began to move away from the concept of rehabilitation. It was costing money, but the upside to that is that the people who benefitted from those programs did not come back to prison.

In my work, I am most proud of being able to help the family members and friends of people who are incarcerated. I think that one of the things that sticks out for me from a personal perspective is a lady I worked with who lived in Florida. Her daughter is serving a life sentence in Maryland and she used to call me to talk for 30 or 40 minutes at a time. She would share how she appreciated the work we were doing to help her daughter. All she wanted was for her daughter to be released before she died, and since she was getting up in age she wasn't able to come up to visit her daughter anymore. During these conversations I listened more than I spoke, and she always told me that she appreciated my willingness to listen. Those types of things are the things that I'm proud of when I'm talking to a mother, wife, daughter, girlfriend, or any family member for that matter about their hopes for their loved one. Those are the things that are important to the work that we do — when we are able to assist family members with things they are going through and for them to really have a sense of hope and be appreciative of the work.

I developed a motto many years ago that I would never give up and I would never give in because I always felt that I would get out of prison. I didn't know when and I didn't know how, but I always felt in me that I would. I saw a lot of those around me give up, lose their minds, and — sometimes — lose their lives. I saw people who were still alive physically, but psychologically and emotionally they were gone. I saw a lot of that, which made me even more determined to fight. I fought the system for so long and so hard that it got to a point where people began to say, "That ni*** ain't never going to get out of jail, not the way he fights the system." So when I was released people began to think if he can get out of prison, then anybody can get out of prison. It was good to know that my release gave others hope, although I always knew in my heart and mind that I was going to get out and be free.

# BOOK THREE
# WISDOM FROM THE INSIDE

OUR HUMAN COMPASSION BINDS US THE ONE TO THE OTHER – NOT IN PITY OR PATRONIZINGLY, BUT AS HUMAN BEINGS WHO HAVE LEARNT HOW TO TURN OUR COMMON SUFFERING INTO HOPE FOR THE FUTURE.
– NELSON MANDELA

# INTRODUCTION
## To THE THIRD BOOK
## BETTYE BLAZE

It's been ten years since I first came up with the idea for this book. I was coming back by myself from visiting Terrence in the prison one time and I was like, I'm going to write a book and I'm going to call it "Doing Time With My Son." When Terrance called me that night, like he did every night, I told him my idea for the book and the name. I remember saying, "We're going to tell your story and how your story affected me and then we're going to talk to some men in there and ask them for some pieces of advice. And then we're going to get their mothers to share some of their thoughts with us too." And from that one idea and that single conversation, here we are.

I felt that it was important to collect these stories so that young men who may have been at-risk to do something wild or crazy could get some first-hand insight of what's going on in the prison and for the mothers who might read this to read from women who might have gone through something similar to what they're going through – so that they would know that they're not alone and that there are so many other mothers out there who have gone through, and are still going through, life every day with a son behind bars.

When Terrence started telling some of the other guys who were in with him about this book idea, they were pumped. Some of them had already been there fourteen years or longer. They were eager to share with me, in their own words, what they had learned and what they wish they had known and what they hoped that other young men would hear so that they wouldn't walk down the same path.

The writings started arriving in the mail and as I started reading, I knew that I needed to reach out to other men in other facilities. So I got some of his other friends who were at other facilities and I called their moms and I asked them if they'd be willing to share their experiences.

What a lot of the mothers said is that what they wrote to me were letters that they should have written to their sons early on in their sentences because they felt like what their sons did often felt like what they did wasn't affecting anyone accept them. These mothers said that they just wished they would have let their sons know the effects of their incarceration on their families — not just financially, but also emotional. For example, some of the women with younger children talked about the sacrifice of spending Saturdays not doing things with their younger children, but carting them to and from the jail for family visits.

I also talked with some mothers who I had met and became friends with in the waiting room during the weekly visits to visit Terrence. Since Terrence was a bit older than many of the other guys, that also meant that their mothers were younger. I took on a bit of a mama role and I think a lot of them looked up to me. For example, I started picking them up if they needed a ride out to the jail. I also kept extra shirts in my car so if their shirts were too low cut, I had a shirt for them. Every one of the mothers I connected with in that waiting room left an impact on me — and

## INTRODUCTION

I still know what many of them are up to to this day.

If you are reading this and you have a son, I really encourage you to involve yourself with reading some of the messages from the inmates and also sharing that with your son. I think the stories that follow present some amazing opportunities to start – or continue – the difficult and necessary conversations. My hope is that out of some of the voices on the pages that follow, you're able to not only read the words on the page, but share them. If you know a young man who is not all the way out there, we have a great chance of making sure that they know there's a chance of showing them something different. We really can do this. It's possible.

**EDITOR'S NOTE**: *We left the letters that follow unedited and unembellished, because there is beauty in the rawness of their words. And because we know there's ample opportunities all around us to hear other people's narratives about Black and Brown men serving time. These are their voices, from the inside, without commentary or apology, in all their beauty and wisdom and pain.*

# 1
# DON'T BELIEVE THE HYPE, JAIL IS STILL JAIL

As an institution, our penal and "correctional" system is an abject failure. The conditions in American jails and prisons virtually ensure psychological impairment for thousands of men and women. It was not until the nineteenth century that the use of prison became widespread. European penology was motivated principally by punishment and retribution. Nowhere in the equation was reform even an option.

My young Black brothers due to the lack of a proper education, due to our economic position in this order of things, these places were built with us in mind. (Note to the Black mothers who have warriors trapped in prison; do not succumb to the backward sympathy of denying us the love and support that's needed in order to teach us a lesson. We need y'all!)

Unlike most of my peers, I had the balance of both parents in my life. What was told to me was either I stop what I was doing, or I would either die, i.e. get killed, or spend the rest of my life in prison. I wish I would have listened to my parents.

SALIH A. JABBAR, 32 YEARS OLD, SERVING 50 YEARS AT M.C.T.C. HAGERSTOWN

# 2
# THE KEY TO STAYING OUT OF PRISON

To all my little young brothers and sisters, one of the most important keys to staying out of prison is to love yourself and respect yourself. Now, you probably wonder why I made that statement, which is good. Well, how many of you tell your parents that you love them as well as your children? Just think for one minute. Because if you do not love yourself, how can you honestly say that you love someone else. Before I was able to understand the reasons for my actions, I had to first learn about myself, which took years of incarceration.

My goal is to help keep the youth out of prison, so please listen to these words real closely. When you're doing whatever you do out there, are you doing it for you or to impress your friends? See, I like to get straight to the core of the problem because a lot of us do not know what a real friend is, which is a shame. Since I have been incarcerated my (mother) has shown me the true meaning of a friend. I also give praise to my Creator because in my time of need He kept me strong and believe me you will get weak at times. Being in prison and on the streets are two different worlds. In prison, you're told what to eat, when to sleep, and at times how to think, so ask yourself is this the life you want?

Your Creator gave you the freewill to choose right from wrong, so apply it to your life and stop playing the blame game because you're in control of you...that is until you give the prison system the power, and then you're nothing but a number. We must remember that our parents are incarcerated with us while we are doing this time because if we do not we will start to lose focus on what is right and what is wrong. This is just the surface of what you will have to deal with, the rest is internal, which means you will be fighting your own demons. The children are the key to the future, which means it is time for you young brothers and sisters to step up and be responsible, or are you scared of responsibility? These are questions that I wish someone would have asked me while I was coming up. So it is an honor to be able to ask these questions to our youth today.

"As a man thinketh so shall he be." This quote is so true and I believe that we all have great potential to be what we want in life. I also believe that we are scared to try our hardest because of failure, which is nothing but a learning experience. I pray that my son, Tony, Jr., does the right things in life because life is just too short not to enjoy it. The old saying goes, "like father like son." Well, I disagree because you still have a chance to learn as well as be something good in life. Just have a little gratitude and I trust and believe that each and everyone of you will be successful.

Most importantly, I trust that I have said something that will at least save one life, which is my duty as a man. If you have read this, I ask that you take the time to just ask yourself what is your life worth, and I hope and pray that you come up with a positive answer.

BRO. ANTONIO HARRIS-EL, 37 YEARS OLD
SERVING 30 YEARS AT M.C.T.C. HAGERSTOWN

# 3
# WHO IS SHE

She carried us in the womb for nine months

Nursed us to our feet, worked hard to make things neat,

Lied and cheat to make sure we eat. WHO IS SHE?

Education was a must, would hoop and holla if we missed the bus. She had one plan and that was to raise a man. WHO IS SHE?

She knew she couldn't compete with the mean streets we had to meet, she encouraged us to hold our heads up no matter how scared, as we took the wrong path, that she knew wouldn't last. WHO IS SHE?

Long days and worried nights she couldn't help to wonder, if she would lose her son to the night. WHO IS SHE?

She had our back no matter how hard it got. She held onto the plan that her baby boy would grow into a man. WHO IS SHE?

She was never ashamed as they called my name, shackled and chained, right or wrong I could always find comfort in her loving arms. This world wouldn't be right if she didn't fuss and fight. WHO IS SHE?

She's my MOM and I miss her loving arms.

BRIAN RAFIQ BLACKSON, SR.
M.C.T.C. HAGERSTOWN

# 4
# MASTER YOUR EGO

Look around for those brothers you once admired; those that are either dead or in prison, and with utmost urgency master your emotions and put your egos in check. Many lives have been lost to the system and graveyard because of emotions that have run rampant when a cooler head would have revealed that the situation could be solved in another fashion.

In retrospect, I can't recall anyone taking time out (a parental figure) to give me a word of advice, and the only word given to me then was "don't do this, or don't do that." Whether that is enough advice for a young man entangled in a destructive lifestyle is anyone's guess.

**MAURICE SMITH, 35 YEARS OLD**
**SERVING 30 YEARS AT A MARYLAND CORRECTIONAL FACILITY**

# 5
# LIFE IS SHORT

My name is Wayne D. Smith, Sr., and this is my life. I was born on September 9, 1973 at 2:48 a.m. By age three, I was living in the deep south of Alabama. Life was hard picking cotton and raising farm animals, which is what I did in Alabama. I can remember playing with the pigs, chickens and wild kittens. At the age of five, we had to leave due to my mother's lack of respect for her husband. She was young in age and wild at heart.

One day I walked in on her sitting on my stepfather's friend leg and I can say "that's when my life changed." By me being a child and all, I told on her, so we had to leave. She had to leave my youngest brother behind when we moved to the next place, which was the fast city called Baltimore. I didn't know that I was born there until the age of nine.

All through my life I was a so called "Black Sheep" of the family. I started school late do to a speech problem, so that was a big problem with me having friends. I was later adopted by a lady named Ms. Rose because my mother was too sick. My mother went through a stage of deep depression and she tried to commit suicide at the age of twenty-four. Really, I was taken from my mother.

Ms. Rose took me to New York for awhile where I went to military school. I was so out of hand that she was afraid that someone would kill me. I stole cards, shoes, money and anything that I wanted. At the age of fourteen, I was locked up and sent to a place called Boys Village for six months. I felt alone but not afraid.

My mother finally got herself together and got me back when I was sixteen. She was doing good for herself. My father wasn't in the picture too much so I can't talk about him. My grandmother was the first lady that broke my spirit. She was a "God-fearing woman" as they say. She knew the Bible. She lived the Bible, and she spoke the Bible. Her name was Mary-Francis Sherrod. She died in 1997. She tried to keep me off of the streets of Baltimore when I moved back from New York, but her efforts failed because when I was eighteen I was arrested for selling drugs. That hurt my grandmother real bad. She would always say, *"Doing things in the dark shall come to the light."*

At the time, I didn't understand what my grandmother meant when she'd say that, but she broke it down like this: Only the devil works in darkness. But what he do will surely show in the light like brand new money. In my words, "Don't do dirt, because you will always feel, be, do and act dirty until you do right." That saying stuck with me for awhile. All the things I have done in my life to girls, family and friends is all coming back on me all at once.

Now, I don't have nobody but myself in here. I don't see my children like I want. I can't go where I want. I can't do what I want. This is just like being a slave, again. My advice to my "son" and other youth is don't do dirt, because it hurt.

When I was first arrested it was the first time I felt really alone. I didn't know anyone. I was thinking that they was going to kill me. It was a older man that showed me that it was more to life than selling drugs and killing. He showed me respect and put me on a mission to save others. I hope that this message saves someone.

WAYNE SMITH, SR., 32 YEARS OLD
SERVING 10 YEARS

# 6

The streets is one big lie. Keep your enemies close and watch your homies. Stay in school. Stay away from fake, phony homies, and be patient.

JOSEPH L. BENNETT, 32 YEARS OLD
SERVING 15 YEARS AT M.C.T.H. HAGERSTOWN

# 7
# IT'S AS SIMPLE AS...

Find two things legally that you enjoy doing in life; think about or ask about how to make these things into a career for yourself. Last and most important, keep a savings account; add to this account seven percent of what you earn a week.

CHRIS BRITTINGHAM, 28 YEARS OLD
SERVING 20 YEARS AT PATUXENT INSTITUTION

# 8

# LIVE A GREAT LIFE

First and foremost, I would like to stress that there are consequences for everything. There is so much more to life than "thuggin." It's all about choices. The choices you make now will determine your future. You have to want more for yourself. So many young Black men see prison as a "rites of passage." There is a miseducation in the hood that prison is a place where you become a man when in reality prison is a dark place that drains your soul; a place where life passes you by.

Men create their own conditions. So many young Blacks limit themselves and place themselves within boundaries that they create. There is so much more to live for. You don't have to be a product of your environment. My life is filled with pain that is and was self-inflicted. I embrace my pain and keep it up front, though. It's sad to say that the only thing that made me change is my pain!

The life of a gangsta leads to death, prison, or addiction to drugs. In order for any person to be successful he needs an education! Opportunities are endless through education. If any person continues to put himself at risk through street life, failure is the only option. This I know from experience.

Every person has to live with regrets. Don't let your regrets rob you of greatness. I'm a firm believer that a faith-based person is a successful person! So I would compel anyone to seek Jesus; there lies your peace! Many young Blacks don't know their fathers so the only male role model they may know is the hustler. They see this lifestyle as being glamorous. They see violence as a way to earn respect. These perceptions are untrue. We can't be deceived by negative images.

Music and television play a role in presenting falsehood. Young men you must face life on life's terms. Your reality must be rooted and grounded in truth. You can't live in a fantasy world wanting to be the next big drug dealer or gangsta. Prisons and graveyards are flooded with men just like you. Learn from those before you. Avoid unnecessary pain.

Coming from the ghetto, I know that many inner city youth live in poverty. There are however other means to provide for your family. Don't let your circumstances be an excuse. It all starts in your mind. Believe in yourself and what you can accomplish! Set goals for yourself. Be mindful of all those who failed before you. A wise man learns from a fool's mistakes. There is nothing slick about being a thug. Actually, it displays a person who has a lack of knowledge.

Take pride in yourself, your family and your community. Instead of tearing down your community, build it up. Learn about your history as a Black man in this country. It will change your identity! Get a sense of self worth. Recognize how valuable you are. Be willing to do some things that you've never done before in order to be someone that you've never been before! This means you have to go through something to be somebody.

Embrace all the hurt and disappointment you've caused yourself and your family. Let that be motivation for you to make positive achievements. Realize that life is hard enough with God; why make it harder without HIM! Seek knowledge and pursue education. Empower yourselves and achieve greatness through positivity. Do what you must to gain success and to be prison free. Jail is no place for a king!! I wish I could have done a lot of things differently, but the one thing that stands out the most is to LISTEN TO ADVICE!

VASUNLALA IRVIN, 30 YEARS OLD
SERVING 22 YEARS AT M.C.T.C.

# 9

# YOU MIGHT GET AWAY AT FIRST

I want to let you young Black brothers know that prison isn't fun, cool or anywhere anyone should be. But, the fact is that most prisons in Maryland are filled with a majority of young Black brothers. In a lot of movies I see how they make prison look, but I know what it's really like cause I'm really here.

Once I started taking a negative path and ending up in court, etc. my family members—including my mother, grandma, and uncles would try to prevent it by talking to me and I would listen but at the same time I had my so-called friends putting negative things in my ear. Unfortunately, I leaned more towards the negativity because I was very young and figured I would never get caught.

I was a straight A student that ended up not going to school which caused me to get into more trouble. I got locked up at the age of thirteen twice, but I got off with a slap on the wrist. My mom figured I'd learn from that, but it only made me try to be smarter in my negative behavior to prevent getting caught again.

I got away with so much it seemed impossible that I'd get caught again. I rebelled to everyone who tried to prevent me from leading that street life. As a result, I got locked up at the age of fourteen and was charged as an adult. Now, I am eighteen years old, serving a twelve year sentence, with four years in and in that four years I have learned a lot about myself, the mistakes I made, and how to prevent those mistakes in the present and future.

Although it wasn't my mistakes that got me locked up the last time, the fact remains that I still made the same mistakes over and over without learning from them. It's a shame that being locked up and serving a twelve year sentence is my learning lesson, but I don't want it to be years. Use my prison experience as yours without having to come here. Believe me, I know it's hard out there, but if you love your life and freedom you would do whatever it takes to stay out of prison, because prison takes freedom from you.

Another thing that makes me not want to come back to jail are the ones that love me. I seem to be hurting them as much as I'm hurting myself, so to solve two problems I could use the time I'm here to improve myself and develop a way to go home and stay home. You have a chance to change before coming to prison, some people don't. So be smart and figure out what you want to do in life.

MARCUS "CAINE" ANDERSON, 18
SERVING 12 YEARS AT M.C.T.F.

# 10
# LISTEN, YOU DON'T HAVE ALL THE ANSWERS

Value family. Why? Because when you are incarcerated your family and loved ones are doing the time with you. Keep yourself or your child involved in activities, i.e. sports, education, recreational leagues. Idle time is the devil's workshop. Focus on school because you are only a kid once and when you become an adult life's decisions are more difficult but are easier when you can make an educated decision.

Also, remember respect is earned not given. When you carry yourself in a respectful manner it is usually given back. Furthermore, choose your friends carefully and don't be a follower if you know they are doing something wrong. To be in the "in" crowd you don't have to do the negative things that they are doing.

As a youth, we think we know all the answers, however, we don't. Listen to your parents because they know more than we give them credit for. The prisons and graveyards are filled with "know it all youngins".

**WAYNE LAMPKIN, 35 YEARS, SERVING 5 YEARS AT MCI-H**

# 11
# DON'T DO IT

Nothing is worth risking your freedom or your life for. Stay in school. Strive toward positive goals. Prison is not cool and no matter how crowded it gets, there is always room for one more person. Interested...?

HAROLD ROGERS, 40 YEARS OLD
SERVING 30 YEARS AT MCTC

# 12

Educate yourself. I say this because education is wisdom and wisdom is power! With these words being put to use you will make it, because you and only you are in charge of your destiny.

STANLEY GWYNN, 37 YEARS OLD
SERVING 15 YEARS AT MCI-H

# 13
# HEED THE ADVICE

Young Black man, please value your freedom! Prison is today's modern day slave ship and it's full of young Black men leaving our precious Black women alone in the struggle called life. This is no life to live for young Black kings. In spite of the myth that they brainwash us to believe, we can survive without killing one another with drugs, guns and violence.

I wish I had taken the advice to not rush to be an adult, stay in school, and enjoy my youth. Not to do drugs and to be a leader rather than a follower to fit in, because now I know that's it's best to stand alone then to fall as a group.

In prison where I am now, you have someone telling you when to eat, sleep, move, even when to think and what to think twenty-four hours a day, seven days week, three hundred sixty-five days a year! Your life no longer belongs to you. Prison is an industry which breeds more violent individuals to maintain the prison capacity at a high level to produce a large income for those who control the powers that be.

If that's not bad enough, your family also becomes a prisoner out of love for you. Your mother becomes shackled out of love and put through degrading searches...physical and otherwise just to see her baby in control by forces beyond her motherly love.

In all, young Black men prison is no place to be not even for one minute of your life, your mother's life, or the lives of those you love. Think Black man and be free!

Peace be upon all the families of all men of color suffering through a loved one's incarceration.

JOSEPH STOKES III, 35 YEARS OLD
SERVING 3 YEARS AT MCI-H

# 14
# IT AIN'T A JOKE

I want all my young brothers and sisters to know that there is a desperate need to try and wake you all up before you all reach that point of self destruction. Too many of you young brothers and sisters are throwing your lives away like I have. Just think about sons and daughters (if you have any) and how they may end up because of your actions.

I was always told I had a good head on my shoulders and that I had the quality to do or become whatever I wanted to in life. Unfortunately, I did not take heed to that advice. Instead, I let myself be sucked into the underworld of crime and I sincerely regret every minute of it.

I would like to quickly address what I am about to say to all my young brothers and sisters out there that may be starting to lead a life of crime. I want to begin by telling you a little bit of my story in hopes that it may deter you from marching down the same road as I have.

I'm James and I am presently doing time (25 years without the possibility of parole) for armed robbery and kidnapping. I started off like some of you perhaps are starting off. I got into trouble as a juvenile. I was hard headed. Didn't want to listen to anyone because I just knew that I had all the answers and solutions to everything I got myself into. Yes sir, I knew what I was doing! I was never going to get caught at anything I did—so I thought. But eventually I did start getting caught and was sent away to the juvenile justice system.

At the same time, I thought that those places were a joke. You know Training School, Boys Village, Montrose where the girls are sent, "huh," I thought I was in heaven in those places just like you may think that most of these juvenile facilities are a playground. But see this is what I want you to understand, this is not the road to take, because real quick it starts to become a revolving door and then that door closes.

I know first hand because my door has already shut. I started just like most of you. I wanted to lie, cheat, steal, get high and take things that didn't belong to me. But now I'm paying the piper. I'm paying for not listening to my parents when they were trying to instill in me to grow up and have a positive, honest character. I'm paying for not listening to those juvenile counselors when they were trying to help me understand that there are better ways to achieve my goals in life.

See, I went on to think that I could get away with anything that I did. (But as you can see that didn't happen.) Oh yeah, and let me tell you I came from a home where I was told "you don't do this" or "you don't do that" or your ass is going to end up in jail. But I didn't listen! So let me tell you the ultimate price I had to pay, and yes I'm still paying it.

Well, first of all, its two decades of my life spent behind bars, watching my son, aunt, sister, and numerous cousins all die while I was incarcerated. I wasn't even allowed to attend their funerals or see them put to rest. Also, not having the opportunity to see my youngest son grow up was difficult. He was one year old when I was arrested, now he's almost a man. Then I watched my so called friends just disappear out of my life. Oh, they may be there for a minute but eventually they will disappear.

I'm letting you know this because I want you to know that there's a big price to pay when you continue to use that revolving door and get into trouble. Eventually, it's going to shut up on you and you are going to end up here where I am. It's not a wonderful place to be, trust me. I'm not going to get into the dangerous things that happen in here, but check this out, more often than not someone gets stabbed or even killed for something that's so small they probably could have just talked about it. Yet most of the time it's not going to happen that way because it's "dog eat dog" in here.

Well, I hope that what I've said will touch someone and open their eyes so that they will not continue to be blind. But just in case there are some of you who do want to keep getting in trouble and using that revolving door, you will be able to walk the yard with me real soon; I promise you that.

I really hope that what I've said will help someone change their minds about a life of crime. The last, but not the least thing I would like to say to you is this, because this is where I've learned to get my salvation from: If you feel that you need help beating the odds, I'm going to share a little secret with you. Pick up your Bible and Jesus will show you the right way to go about anything that you may have trouble with in your life.

This is also something that I know first hand, because without the help of Jesus I don't know how I would have handled all the drama that I have had in my life. But with His help I have been able to overcome the complex situations of my life. Young brothers and sisters I just want you all to know that if you are having troubles with anything in your life don't be afraid to ask your parents or someone that you trust to help you.

These words go out to all my young brothers and sisters out there. If this story applies to you, please clean yourself up before it's too late.

**JAMES CLARK, 44 YEARS OLD**
**SERVING 25 YEARS WITHOUT PAROLE**

# 15
# IT'S ALL ABOUT YOU

Don't allow your peers or environment to dictate who you are as an individual. Never let anyone tell you what you can and cannot do. Always be a leader and never follow the footsteps of another person. Education is power and with some sort of education, nothing is impossible!

MATTHEW JONES, 21 YEARS OLD
SERVING 16 YEARS M.C.T.C.

# 16
# REALITY CHECK

Young people, believe what I say when I tell you that this place called jail is for losers. Ain't nothin' slick about coming here. It's real easy to get here and it gets harder to get out. After awhile it gets harder once you're released to start over time and time again because you lose everything.

JESSE REID, 36 YEARS OLD
SERVING 7 YEARS AT MCI-H

# 17
## GAME OVER

Life is beautiful, full of promise, possibilities and potential. Prison exhausts these promises, possibilities, and potential...turning life ugly and not worth living. Why subject yourself to such an experience? Everyone in prison will tell you if they had to do it all again they would do it different and avoid prison! Life is not a game or sport. However, if you are foolish enough to look at it that way then consider prison GAME OVER!

MICHAEL BOYER, 33 YEARS OLD
SERVING 50 YEARS AT WESTERN CORRECTIONAL INSTITUTION

# 18
## AND IT GOES LIKE THIS...

If you're living a life of crime—plain and simple, either you're going to end up dead or in jail. I know you may have heard this a thousand times, but nobody never gave it to you like this. Ride with me young pimp, open your ears up, and soak this game up.

Let's say you came up in the game, things are going good—at least in your mind. You have the finest woman in town. You drive the big cars and take trips all around the world. I mean things is going good for you. This is the best you ever done in your life. You doing things you only read about. The whole town is looking up to you. But don't get comfortable young pimp, because here comes the flip side. Someone is always waiting in the wings while you're doing your thing.

You have the guys who just wanna kill you because they want your money or your fame. We call them haters. Then you have the jealous ones that feel as though you are in their way. To eliminate you they have to rat you out (snitch). Then you have the females that you think are on your side. They are the worst, because you expose so much to them that you end up not being able to just cut them off. So you try to feed them with a long handle spoon, and of course that's not enough, because they want their cake and eat it too.

I ain't finished yet, let's not forget your "man;" the one you grew up and threw up with. I know you're saying not my man. But ask yourself, have I ever really tested his/her friendship? It's easy to roll with a winning team. But truth be told, the streets lie. They only want to use and abuse you. And even though y'all grew up and threw up together, ask yourself, why would he die for me? Do you really believe that he will let you go free while he stays in jail? Do you really believe that he will let his family starve for the love of you? Do you really believe he has your back when it ain't benefiting him? Ask yourself.

Young pimp, let me hip you to something. Niggas is rolling with the highest bidders (major players). I know you're saying not my man. Yes, your man. If you think I'm lying put him to the test, because a soldier never knows his strength until he's put to the test...until he's challenged. Let your back get against the wall and you are in a box where you can barely move. All your homies will bounce and leave you. That's when you have to call on your true friends that you treated so bad; you know the ones you pushed so far out of your life because they refused to be apart of your foolishness.

Now, everything that they tried to keep you away from, they have to fight to help you get out of...all because of love. These are the ones who really have your back no matter what you have done or can do, because it was never about that with them in the first place. But ask yourself, why should they lend a helping hand when you done them so wrong. Funny thing is you were so caught up in worldly things you didn't even see it all coming. Now you are sitting behind the wall talking and walking the year reminiscing about how things used to be. Damn, young pimp!

JOSEPH L. BENNETT

# 19
# MY DAMASCUS ROAD EXPERIENCE

My name is Leo Coleman, Jr. My heart's desire is to reach young men and women and youth whom the devil is trying to kill and destroy. I thank God for transforming my life out of a life of drugs, alcohol, and incarceration. This is only to name a few of the things God has delivered me from, but there were many more.

I was somewhat like the prodigal son who thought the world had more to offer me than my loving family and my God. I was raised up in the household with a mother and a father, which later became one parent, my mother. I was bitter and hurt knowing that my father was no longer a part of my life so I rejected God whom I was raised up to love and respect and then I went out into a world that was full of pain and suffering—thus began my life of incarceration.

My first imprisonment was at the age of sixteen which only grew into upscale periods of crime and incarceration. I had lived incarceration the majority of my youth until the age of thirty-six. My incarceration was a period of twenty long years of in and out. Not one time in all of that period of incarceration did I think about God. My only concern was how much money my mother was sending me from home.

While incarcerated I started riots, attempted riots, and was steady trying to reach a goal of becoming a lifer—not knowing that God loved me more than the way I was behaving; that is until my night of transformation. I was released from prison in June of 1980. I was a free man physically, but still incarcerated in my mind. And so I picked up my lifestyle of doing wrong and bearing corrupt fruit. I went into the church to rob somebody because this is where the devil told me I could obtain some money to support my drug demon. Although it was a trap set by the devil, I had a Damascus experience at this point and ended up seeing myself as the sinner I am and made a promise to turn away from my deathful lifestyle and ask Jesus to save me a wretch like me.

And guess what? Jesus saved me right where I was. All I had to do was confess and believe. Now I am living my life for the Lord and since God has given me a ministry of reconciliation I now go back in the prison to preach Jesus. I am in prison ministry with Christian Life Kingdom Ministries. My home church is Simmons Memorial Baptist Church.

I realize today that I'm just a servant with a message of life. I feel like Joshua. I'm prepared to lead you out of the wilderness. I feel like Jeremiah. God's word is shut up in my bones like fire and I can't keep it to myself. I feel like Isaiah when he said, "Lord here am I send me." But I told the Lord myself I don't care where you want me to go, I'll go.

I thank God for all that I've been through. I have no regrets for my lifestyle, because out of it I have a legitimate testimony, and the only person who can give you a legitimate testimony is God Himself. I am crucified with Christ, nevertheless the life I now live I live by faith of the Son of God who loved me and gave Himself for me.

Thank God for Jesus.

LEO COLEMAN, JR., 62 YEARS OLD
SERVING 6 MONTHS TO 6 YEARS AT PENAL FARM HAGERSTOWN

# 20

Go to school and get educated and stay out of the streets!

Simple as that!!

ROLAND A. PERRY, JR., 38 YEARS OLD
SERVING 9 YEARS AT M.C.T.C.

# 21
# SUCCESS AND DREAMS

In order for one to embrace success he must first be formally introduced to failure. For failure is only a temporary setback in your travels toward success. Keep your dreams in front of you so you can see them clearly, which encourages you to follow them wholeheartedly. As you follow them wholeheartedly, one day your dream will no longer be a dream for it will become your reality.

DARRIN SCOTT, 38 YEARS OLD
SERVING 15 YEARS AT MCI-H

# 22
## THINK

My beloved brothers, please think about your futures. Please think about the joys and pleasures of freedom. Being able to think for yourself and do for yourself. Please think about your loved ones. Think about the freedom you have to love and be loved without restrictions or conditions set by others. Think about your ability to eat what you want when you want. Think of your ability to go out when you want. My beloved brother, please think because your life depends on it.

I was told by my grandmother and mother that if I didn't grow up and start acting like a young adult, I would be killed or in prison. They were right. After eighteen years of striving to survive in this jungle that is prison, I've come to the realization that I should have listened to my grandmother and mother. Think about what's right and do it. Never let anyone tell you that something wrong is right.

DAVID SMITH, 36 YEARS OLD
SERVING 30 YEARS AT M.C.T.C.

# 23
## MY LIFE

May 12, 1976, at the age of seventeen, I was arrested for first-degree murder and on November 3, 1976 I was sentenced to Life Imprisonment. November 3, 1976 I entered the Maryland State Penitentiary–not yet a man, but forced to become a man that day.

Suffering from peer pressure I come into the Pen running wild, trying to fit in and had my ups and downs–on and off of lock-up for a lot of stupid things.

A friend of my brother's pulled me up and had a talk with me about the way I was headed in my life and that if I did not change my behavior I would spend the rest of my life in prison. This friend (Malik Rahman) become a role model for me and a few other young men that came into the Pen acting crazy. This is the time that I decided to do something positive with my life.

I joined the Scared Straight Program (that later became Project Turnaround) and that is when I became very adamant about helping "at-risk" youth.

I am truly sorry for the pain and suffering that I have caused the victim's family and the pain and suffering that I have caused my own family. My plans when I reach society is to start my own Juvenile Prevention and Alternative Program called CRY (Creating Responsible Youth).

I am now fifty years old. At this point, with thirty plus years of my life spent in prison and thirteen years after I was recommended for pre-release and work release I am still at a medium security prison and cannot advance any further even with all of my achievements. Young people wise up and become a responsible youth.

# EDUCATIONAL ACHIEVEMENTS

General Education Development — GED

Bachelor's Degree in Sociology — Coppin State College

Concentration in Juvenile Group Counseling

Continuing Education and Workforce Development (A.A.C.C.)

Individual Development (Anne Arundel Community College)

Employment Techniques Course (A.A.C.C.)

Clerical Occupation (Hagerstown Junior College)

Basic Electronics Course

# JUVENILE COUNSELING ACHIEVEMENTS

Coppin State College (High Risk Youth Project)

Peer Counseling, Drug Education and Prevention Program

Coppin State College (High Risk Youth Project)

Peer Advocate, Drug Education and Prevention Program

Alternatives to Violence (Basic Course)

Alternatives to Violence (Community Training)
Alternatives to Violence (Facilitator Course)
Social Services Course (15 hours of Group Counseling)
Letter from the Department of Juvenile Justice
Letter from the Department of Juvenile Services
Special Project (Alternative to Sentencing)
Letter from the Alternative to Sentencing Program
Project Turnaround Counselor of the Year
Project CHOICES Counselor (Outstanding Service)
Jaycees Phase One Youth Group Counseling Certificate
Letter from Booker T. Washington Middle School
Letter from Stemmers Run Middle School

KARL D. BROWN AKA KAREEM HASAN

# 24
# NUGGETS OF WISDOM

There's no honor in coming to jail, even the so called toughest want out.

Time has no patience or consideration for anyone or anything.

Don't comfort yourself today to kill yourself tomorrow, like an exploding pillow.

Be mindful of the things you do; who you do them to; who you do them with; when you do them; where you do them; how you do them, and why you do them.

Jail is a slow death—mentally, physically and spiritually.

CRAIG MORRIS, 40 YEARS OLD
SERVING 20 YEARS AT WESTERN CORRECTIONAL INSTITUTION

# 25
## NIGHTLY PRAYER

Lord, I come to you to ask you to bless my family, friends, enemies and my peers,

To watch over them and give them the strength to overcome their fears.

Some are just lost Lord and need your guidance to see the light,

Just like me Lord that's why I pray to you every night.

Forgive us Lord for we all have sinned,

You are our only God, Father and truest Friend.

Without you Lord this world would be through,

That's why when we pray we only pray to You.

I worry about people's future, they just don't have the right plans,

But don't give them no excuse because they know the world is in Your hands.

The Bible, the churches, some don't believe in them at all,

We have an excuse for everything even why the raindrops fall.

Help us all Lord because Satan is beating us with the bat,

I know if we stay strong and have faith you will handle even that.

In the end Lord sinners will have a lot to say,

What was promised to us is coming soon and that's that Judgment Day.

We need you Lord because life isn't like studying for a quiz,

I don't know about everybody else but I'm ready for you to come down here and handle Your bizz (business).

I've changed, turned around, and am also free from sin,

I love you, thank you, and I end this prayer with AMEN!

HAROLD SINGFIELD, 22 YEARS OLD
SERVING 44 YEARS

# 26
## MY SON

The impact of my son being incarcerated has brought overwhelming tears and sadness to the family. As the only son with two sisters, I look at how much he has missed out on – the family gatherings, his son's first day of school, Mother's Day. As a mother, I miss him being around me – the hugs and kisses that he would give me like no other. There's that time of loneliness when I look for him to come walking through my front door any minute. Me sitting in my living room just wondering and thinking to myself, "Lord, my child has never diminished. It has made him love himself and others in a different way than before and I thank God for that."

ANGELA BECOAT
MOTHER TO JAAMAL WEEKS WHO SERVED 5 YEARS AT JESSUP PATUXENT

# 27
# NONE LIKE I HAVE FOR THIS ONE

There have been many a night that I have cried, but none like I have for this child. I gave birth to a beautiful brown bouncing baby boy over 30 years ago and since then I have given birth to him many times over and over and over again. I have been a victim of circumstance... twice.

As a mother, you never want to say these words — my son killed someone. But he did. It's nothing that I am proud of and he isn't either, but it's the truth nonetheless. The pain that I feel for that mother was overwhelming and even more overwhelming that before her death, she never had the chance to forgive my child or maybe she just didn't want to. And I know that to many people a statement that my son made to me at that time doesn't mean much, but it was what I had to hold onto and also what made me feel like he was salvageable. You see, unlike many I know, he accepted that he actually committed the crime. He stated, "Ma, it is nothing that you have done, but I did this all myself." He made that statement after we had turned him over to authorities and after he had confessed to the crime. The burden that I carry from that incident is still heavy, but it has helped me to form the person that I have become and still becoming. And his statement allowed me to breathe and to not blame myself.

Okay, I did say twice, so here it goes. Sometimes I still cry when I remember hearing my 28-year-old son's voice crackling on the phone, crying because he was being accused of a crime that he did NOT commit. It's funny, tears are welling up now and they will probably exist forever. Every time I think of what we subject ourselves to, I think about the choices that we make in our lives that affect others who love us. Those choices dictate our lives personally — directly and indirectly — and every living soul that cares and loves us. A painful thought, but again the truth — even when the choices are ours and even more so when you're simply a victim of a choice that your loved one has made. I smile all the time, but no one really knows. Sometimes uncontrollable tears just present themselves. Still, I smile. My son spent almost three years in prison for a crime that he did not commit. After doing time on the murder charge, coming home, attending college, and teaching at a private school, he was accused of rape. He was acquitted of the charges and still not released because of the original murder charge. And still when you saw me I smiled, crying everyday internally, not always understanding and never agreeing with the decisions that were being handed to me — but still, I smile.

My heart has been trampled upon repeatedly. I couldn't believe that as a taxpayer I was actually paying for the corruption that I saw and had to digest daily in the courtroom, the injustice that I and my family were subjected to in the court of societal opinion. As a woman first and foremost, I was wounded and appalled because any man — my son, my brother, my father, and the list could go on and on — that violates any woman should be punished for the consequences of his actions. Lastly, as a grieving mother missing my son, I felt an emptiness that can only be explained by a mother separated from her child — a longing to rescue, a longing to relieve his pain, a longing to have someone to relive mine. Still, I smile!

DANA BANKINS, MOTHER

# EPILOGUE
## TERRENCE G. WHITE

### FALL 2016

When I started getting in trouble, I lost contact with my paternal grandmother and my aunt. Just last week, his cousin was in the market and overheard these women talking in the grocery store, which led to me finding my grandmother's number and calling her yesterday. My aunt was there too. It was really exciting to reconnect, knowing that I have a better story for her now. I'm bringing back the people I've always wanted in my life, but with whom I didn't want to share what I was doing in that time in my life. Sometimes people let it go until someone dies and I can see now how it would be easy to do that. My grandmother is nearly 80 now and I'm just glad I have a good story to share with her now while she's still alive.

### WINTER 2016

Some people can't understand how I'm as close to my mom as I am, but I'm her only son. And for my whole life it's been me and her. Her and me. We talk every day. I feel like after all these years of me doing the stuff I've done, she deserves to also share in the joy of my life now. These last few years I've been so blessed and I just want her to know everything day-to-day. I just want her to know everything.

## SEPTEMBER 23, 2016

Today, my daughter Shantell gave birth to two beautiful boys, my grandsons. They are the first boys born in my family since the day of my own birth. I have so many hopes for them, so many dreams yet unspoken. But above all else, I hope they grow up knowing that as long as they keep the love in their family strong, as long as they rest on the strength of who they were born to be, who they were destined to become, then anything is possible. Love endures. This I know for sure.

# GRATITUDE

Collectively, we would like to first thank God for putting it on our hearts to share our story with the world. We give thanks to everyone who contributed to this book, especially the guys at the Hagerstown Correctional Facility and other facilities. We thank all of the young men who went through the Youth Challenge Program, most notably those who went through during the time I (Terrence) was a program mentor. My involvement in that program helped save my life. We would also like to thank the administration at the Hagerstown Correctional Facility for allowing David Miller and LaMarr Shields, formerly of the Urban Leadership Institute, to come speak with the young men. Thanks to Miss Allen for helping to make that happen. I (Bettye) also want to thank my church family, Called to Action Ministries, for caring about our family and our struggles. Your prayers gave me strength daily. We would also like to collectively thank Regina Salliey for helping us to design and shape this book in its beginning stages. You knew I (Bettye) couldn't spell, but believed that we had a story that mattered. And to Mischa Toland for getting us started on this journey and encouraging me (Bettye) all those years ago. Mischa, you are my friend, my niece, my child and I love you.

I (Bettye) would like to thank my family who believed that I could get this book done and praised me for not blaming myself for the things Terrence chose to do. I thank Shantell White, Terrence's daughter, for loving her father through this; my two sisters, Jeanne and Joan, who are also two of my best friends, for believing in me; my daughter-in-law Brandee White, for loving and believing in Terrence and for having the strength to weather the storm; Terrence's mother-in-law, Betty Whitaker, and her entire family for loving my son, and a special thanks to Terrence's later father-in-law, Mr. Marcus, who loved Terrence unconditionally, may he rest in peace knowing that his daughter and granddaughters are being taken good care of by my son. To my best friend of 28 years, Sherrie Clark, who has walked every step of the way with me; and to my two nieces, Jeannelle (Tonie) and Dawnita (Dink), who think I am the best aunt in the world. Thank you also to my Urban Leadership Institute family — David Miller, Dr. LaMarr Shields, and Scott Johnson. The years we worked together with ULI meant so much to me. A special thanks to LaMarr for letting me to continue to travel your professional road with you. I love you like my own son and believe deeply in you and in the purpose of your work.

I (Terrence) would like to thank my entire family, especially my two amazing daughters, amazing grandchildren, wife, mother, and all my extended family. Your love is the reason that I am standing today and am able to tell my story at all. I am because we are.

We would also like to collectively thank the team at Full Circle Press for making the writing, editing, and publishing process so wonderful, including the amazing graphic designer Laura and the entire editing team, with special thanks to Savannah Waller for

## GRATITUDE

her work on the interview transcriptions and proofreading. And last but not least, special thanks to one of the coolest, smartest, and most patient women I (Bettye) have ever had the pleasure of calling my friend, Dr. Marina Gillmore, CEO and President of Full Circle Press. I don't even have the words to express my thanks for your work in making this book a reality. It could not have happened without you. After just a couple of weeks into our work together, you made me see how I really did have a story worth sharing, and for that Terrence and I thank you. I know it was a lot of hard work and long nights on your behalf, but I had a blast working hard with you. I can't begin to tell you how much you are appreciated and loved, so I will just tell you that Terrence and I love you to the moon and back. Keep writing and making dreams come true.

Finally, to anyone that we may have forgotten to mention who had anything to do with making this book becoming a reality, we thank you.

# ABOUT THE AUTHORS

**BETTYE L. BLAIZE** is a mother of one son, grandmother of two, and great-grandmother of three who resides in Baltimore, Maryland. She was educated in Baltimore City Schools and continued her education at Strayer Business College, where she studied accounting. She started her career at Holiday Inn as a desk clerk and proudly worked her way up to the position of manager. She retired from the Holiday Inn after 29 proud years of service. Throughout her life, Bettye has had a passion for working with and encouraging young people, and it was this passion that led her to re-enter the workforce after retirement as an administrative assistant with the Urban Leadership Institute in Baltimore. In this role, Bettye managed many daily operations of the company and assisted co-founders David Miller and Dr. LaMarr D. Shields in their work in schools and non-profits throughout the country. She currently serves as the chief administration assistant for the Cambio Group, where she travels nationwide and contributes to the Cambio Group's mission of affecting change at both the individual and systemic level in schools, non-profits, and government agencies. Bettye also works with the SPARK Center for Professional and Personal Renewal, a non-profit organization dedicated to helping teachers, social workers, and other change

## ABOUT THE AUTHORS

agents reignite their passions for their professions. When she's not working or traveling, Bettye loves nothing more than spending time with her incredible family in Baltimore.

**TERRENCE WHITE** is a loving husband to his beautiful wife Brandee White. He is the father of two lovely girls, Shantell and Alayah, and has three amazing grandchildren. He is a devoted husband, father, grandfather, and son whose commitment to his family surpasses all else in his life. Terrence was educated in both Catholic Schools and Baltimore County Schools and although he excelled in school at an early age, he lost his way during his teen years and as a result spent time in several correctional facilities. While locked up, Terrence became a part of a program called Youth Challenge, where he served as a facilitator and mentored young men who faced charges similar to his own. His involvement in this program opened his eyes to the power of mentorship and instilled in him a desire to give back to young men who found themselves involved in the criminal justice system at an early age. During his time, Terrence also earned his plumbing and construction licenses and graduated from these programs with a GPA of 3.7. Upon coming home, Terrence has fulfilled every major goal that he has set for himself, including earning his CDL license and landing a truck driving position with a major company. Terrence resides with his family in the Baltimore area.

# ABOUT FULL CIRCLE PRESS

Full Circle Press is a socially-conscious, purpose-driven independent publishing house with a deep commitment to contributing to the greater good through helping to write, edit, publish and market books that matter. We believe in changing the world one story at a time and we envision a world where quality books and literacy resources are available to all. We are educators at heart and are passionate about teaching what we know, sharing resources when and where we can, and empowering others to do and be better. Visit www.fullcirclepress.org to learn more about our products, programs and services.